Penguin Books
MANLY GIRLS

Born in the Netherlands in 1946, Elisabeth Wynhausen
grew up in Sydney. She is a well known journalist who has
worked for the *Telegraph*, the *Bulletin*, and the *National
Times*. She lives in New York and is a correspondent for
the Melbourne *Age*. This is her first book.

MANLY GIRLS

Elisabeth Wynhausen

Penguin Books

Penguin Books Australia Ltd
487 Maroondah Highway, PO Box 257
Ringwood, Victoria 3134, Australia
Penguin Books Ltd
Harmondsworth, Middlesex, England
Viking Penguin, A Division of Penguin Books USA Inc.
375 Hudson Street, New York, New York 10014, USA
Penguin Books Canada Limited
10 Alcorn Avenue, Toronto, Ontario, Canada M4V 1E4
Penguin Books (N.Z.) Ltd
182–190 Wairau Road, Auckland 10, New Zealand

First published by Penguin Books Australia, 1989
10 9 8 7 6 5 4 3
Copyright © Elisabeth Wynhausen 1989

Typeset in Sabon by Renwick Pride Pty Ltd, Albury, NSW
Made and printed in Australia by Australian Print Group, Maryborough, Victoria

National Library of Australia
Cataloguing-in-Publication data:
Wynhausen, Elisabeth, 1946–
Manly girls
ISBN 0 14 007472 4.
1. Wynhausen, Elisabeth, 1946-   . 2. Immigrants —
New South Wales — Sydney — Biography.
3. Sydney (N.S.W.) — Social life and
customs — 1945 –   I. Title.
994.4104092

CONTENTS

In 1951 Mr J.B. Schoonbeek, then a month short of his 99th birthday, left the Netherlands with his 71-year-old daughter to emigrate to South Africa; asked why he was leaving, Mr Schoonbeek said: 'Because there is no future in the Netherlands'.

ONE
The Workingman's Paradise

We came to Australia by accident. My aunt Ali, the bookworm, read *A Town Like Alice* and convinced the others that Australia was a land of opportunity. With little idea of what to expect, my aunts and uncles shipped the furniture, the Frigidaire and the wash basins to the unknown continent, and went on ahead, quickly writing to say that it never rained in Sydney. Having given away our raincoats, we took off on the long flight. The plane flew by day. At night the passengers were put up at hotels en route, a relief for my mother and father, who had to share their seats because KLM, the stingy Dutch airline, gave small children half-seats for half-price tickets.

Delayed by engine trouble in Darwin, where the temperature was about 40°C, passengers waited all day in the airport, a tin shed in a field of dust. Faintly discouraged, we flew to Sydney. Our arrival, in the second week of January 1951, was recorded for posterity. Uncle Nick, a gregarious man uninhibited by his halting English, had convinced the photographer from the *Sydney Morning Herald* that we were people of some note, and as we stepped on to the tarmac, exhausted, crumpled and irritated, with my three-year-old brother Jules in tears from the shock of landing, the photographer sprang forward and took our picture.

The rain began the following afternoon and kept up for three weeks. The family had arranged for us to stay in a private hotel in Cremorne, north of the Harbour Bridge. Kept indoors

1

because she was ill, my mother stared through the window at a sodden suburban street which always seemed to be deserted. It crossed her mind more than once that it had been a dreadful mistake to talk my father into emigrating. But her spirits picked up when the weather cleared, because we were able to go out exploring.

Dad was knocking on doors. His experience as a cattle dealer seemed to have little relevance to our revised situation. The economy was in a slump and managers sometimes bristled at the very idea of employing the ragtag and bobtail arriving from Europe when decent Australians were out of work. 'Not here, mate,' he'd be told although he had seen the advertisement in the classifieds the same morning, and waited for the place to open, 'there's nothing here.'

The uncles reassured him that it had happened to them as well, but by then, after about three months in Sydney, they were passing themselves off as old hands. Uncle Bram, the older of my mother's two brothers to emigrate, had found work as a salesman for Riverstone, a meat company, and fitted right in, so he said, once he was accustomed to the frequent pauses for refreshment.

It flattered him to be invited to the pub, after only a day at work. Intent on doing the right thing, he matched the others schooner for schooner until he passed out cold. The next morning, he felt much as he had the time he copped a bullet in the temple, illegally crossing a border during the war, but he reappeared at the crack of dawn. 'This is the first stop,' said the man who was supposed to be showing him the ropes, and they went into a pub near the markets for a beer or two. The idea was that Bram was meant to memorize his route. What with the schooners they had at lunch, he hardly remembered his own name, and he had to stifle a shudder of horror when someone suggested a drink after work. Summoning up the vestiges of his considerable self-discipline, he agreed; it was not in his nature to let himself fail a test, and he had already heard contemptuous comments about the types who shirked their shift at the pub. In fact his co-workers soon went out of their way to exclude him from the running commentary on the wogs.

'You Dutchies are orright,' a driver for Riverstone told him after they had exchanged about three words. 'You don't stick together like them dagoes.'

Unable to find a steady job at first, my father took almost anything that came along. One day he went door-to-door in bucolic Camden, sixty miles south-west of the city, with a suitcase full of ladies' undies. Despite Camden's legendary shortage of lingerie, he did not make his mark as a travelling salesman. He did not have much in the way of salesman's patter and his English failed him altogether the final time he flung open his suitcase to hold up a lacy half-slip rumoured to have been a best seller from Penrith to Picton, because he caught a roguish wink from the middle-aged woman who stood at the door — in a housecoat. '... Elastic,' he said, tugging at it, 'good elastic ...'

'I don't see what's so funny,' he shouted, the following evening, enraged because mum and the uncles were exaggerating the incident as they compared notes. Supplied with goods by another of our so-called connections in the rag trade, Uncle Nick had sold handbags to shops in Sydney, clearing out the stock in a matter of days. He had the nerve to return a month or two later with fresh samples and shopkeepers, still smarting at their own gullibility, threw him out.

'I still have a couple of those bags,' he said innocently, 'what was that address in Camden again, Paul?'

'Listen, Nico,' said dad in Dutch, stabbing the air with his finger, 'we've heard enough of your twaddle ...'

'He's right,' Uncle Bram chipped in, 'if that dame goes for the good-looking type, Nico doesn't stand a chance.'

'Don't you start,' said dad. Their banter irritated him. Unable to adjust to its pace, excluded from its complicated intimacy, he felt himself to be the odd man out.

He was a provincial from Heer, in the south of Holland, a

village so cramped in its horizons that brawls used to break out if boys from the south end of the main street risked appearing at the dancehall in the north end, two kilometres away. The people he had known as a lad did not resolve a difference by laughing it off. Quick with his fists, or whatever came to hand, he continued to delight in the memory of his own recklessness. Even as an adult he flared at imagined slights and he always rose to the bait.

'The apartment's starting to look cosy,' said one of the aunts, 'but it might be better if you hang that painting over there, above the sideboard.'

'Yes, maybe so,' said mum, doubtless deciding privately not to change a thing. We had just moved into a flat on the main road in Balgowlah, on the north side of Sydney, and my parents were still telling other Dutch people about going to see the owner of the building, a woman who spoke very rapidly in a broad Australian accent, slowing down only to say that the rent was eight guineas a week. Outside her place, unmindful for once of the tight, disapproving faces of the people passing them by, they stood still and laughed aloud: though they couldn't make head or tail of what she had said, they'd signed the lease nonetheless.

Dutch people were inclined to avoid the 'dirty', cramped inner suburbs and fled instead to the further reaches of suburbia, fencing off gardens done up with miniature windmills where there had been 'nothing' but bush. Our clan had compromised, so to speak, settling in the middle distance. The aunts and uncles lived for a time in Mosman, an old, well-to-do district some five or six miles from the city. The owner of the house assumed that he was renting it to Bram and Ali, and their little boy, my cousin Ron. Mosman was a nice sort of place, he told them again and again. Not a lot of strangers. People knew each other. They took an interest. What he seemed to be saying, according to Uncle Bram, was that he did not want the neighbours complaining that the house was swarming with foreigners, and luckily he never learned that he had a few more tenants than he had bargained for, because Nick and his wife Nan had moved in at midnight, on the sly. They panicked if someone approached. Nick excitedly shouted instructions at his wife. He in turn was told off by his brother, and they were interrupted by Ali, who had kept watch from behind a curtained window. People who knocked on the door may have puzzled over the peculiar scuffling sounds as Nick and Nan rushed off to hide under the double bed.

Unable to do much about the decor of the big, dark house in Mosman, the aunts were taking an insistent interest in our flat. 'Yes, I like it too,' Aunty Nan said, 'though I still think that material you put over the sofa could have been a little darker.'

'Chacun à son goût,' said mum brightly, going on without any change of tone, 'did I tell you about the lottery ticket with the girls at work? We won twenty pounds and celebrated immediately with a bottle of wine. I felt like a real Australian, sipping wine as if I didn't have a care in the world.'

She was employed as a machinist, at a small bedding factory in the city. The other women had gone out of their way to help her, the only foreigner, pretending not to notice if she came to work with reddened eyes after crying on the long bus ride, imagining that she could still hear Jules who howled with anguish at being left at kindergarten.

'I had the wine, and I was just thinking how nice to put a few extra pounds in my pocket, but they spent the rest of the money on more lottery tickets.'

'Echt Australian, heh,' said Uncle Nick.

'Well, of course, you'd know . . .'

'Stop it, Paul,' said mum, smoothing over the material on the couch with an air of satisfaction, before she stood up and spoke in English. 'So, who vants coffee?'

That week, or the next, dad started as a salesman at David Jones and, as soon as we dared, we dressed up to go to the David Jones emporium on George Street, in the city, just to see him at work. The department store was an enchanted realm that tempted all the senses. Aromatic smells from the food hall in the basement wafted through the ground floor. Packages mysterious with newness were piled up on the counters. Clasped firmly by the hand, Jules and I dug in by the elevator, never having seen its like before, and confirmed our astonishment in each other's faces as mum hurried us off to the tie department.

'Look, look,' we whispered, unwilling to draw attention to ourselves, unsure how to contain the excitement of seeing dad in so remote and significant a role, 'there he is . . .' He stood talking to an important-looking man who wore a white carnation in his buttonhole. We couldn't take our eyes off him, but mum pretended to be a customer, holding up some ties until at last he saw us and came over. Worried about our getting him into trouble, I kept glancing around, but it was all right, because mum appeared to be consulting him about a dark red tie, and we left in a minute or two without anyone having noticed.

On the way back along George Street, we were caught in the eddy of a crowd waiting for a tram. 'They're from Australia,' said Jules, almost under his breath, awed at seeing so many of them at once.

'Those ladies over there all have hats and gloves,' I whispered, and the two of us exploded into giggles. Usually we pretended that the natives were identical to us, in case they thought we were being rude about them.

'Perhaps they think it's cold,' mum said softly, looking up to smile pleasantly at perfect strangers. 'Ah, here is paps . . .'

'We saw you at work, papa,' I said.

'In there,' added Jules, wriggling around in dad's arms to point. The interior of the department store was deserted. Dustsheets thrown over the counters shone white in the gloom.

My mother had glanced around at the sound of the post office clock. 'In fifteen minutes, the shops will all be dark and the streets will be empty.'

'Empty?' I said wonderingly. The crowd had flowed out around us.

'Completely empty . . .'

We had slewed around a little as dad halted to salute a leathery-looking man who was approaching.

'Nice to see you.'

'That's right,' said the man, nodding at mum as he raised his flat, broad-brimmed hat.

'This is my wife, and these are my children, Betty and Jules.'

'Pleased to meet you.'

'I met this gentleman in David Jones,' dad said eagerly, 'and we talked a little bit about cattle. But he has sheep. Merino sheep . . .'

'That's right,' said the man. 'Well, I better be getting along,' and, raising his hat again, he strode off.

Before we were grudgingly approved as immigrants, my parents were interrogated by Australian officials so intent on ferreting out people with criminal tendencies that dad had to go to the Hague yet again when they turned up an old speeding charge against him. They asked a thousand questions but were unwilling to admit that they had no answers and they left dad with the impression that he could lease a farm outside Sydney to start up again as a cattle dealer. He knew as much about cattle dealing as anyone in South Limburg but that was to be faint consolation.

'You'd need a bloody fortune to go up against the big blokes in the business,' said the first person in Sydney that he asked about it.

The ceaseless rain in the weeks following our arrival flooded the country town of Maitland, north of Sydney. The newspapers had front-page pictures of the disaster. People were being rescued by rowboat from the roofs of outlying buildings and livestock had to be left to drown. Though the Dutch are famous for making polders out of marshland, and draining fields that would otherwise lie under water, my parents were peculiarly disconcerted by the idea of what had happened around Maitland. *A Town Like Alice* had prepared them for almost any climatic oddity, but not, of all things, a flood. Reminded that they knew nothing about the land, they decided to stay in Sydney, for the time being.

Before the end of 1951, they together with Bram and Ali, had bought a house in Lewis Street, Balgowlah, a staid, peninsular suburb between the Spit Bridge and the road to the northern beaches. People of means insisted on calling it Balgowlah Heights and, with suburbia starting to take itself seriously, they prevailed. The minutiae of status seemed to matter. Our bit of the street was less than a quarter of a mile long, but its social scale was precisely calibrated from east to west. To the east of us were gabled, two-storied houses built before the war and half-hidden behind spreading trees, a lush growth we took for a sign of wealth.

Our own unenviable position did not inhibit the local response to us, however, and we were welcomed as the first foreigners to move into the neighbourhood. Up at the local shops, people my mother half-recognized might work a conversation around to the point where they could reassure her that we were a good type of migrant. Perhaps it sounded a little patronizing, but life was complicated enough without making such fine distinctions, and if anything preoccupied my parents it was the precariousness of existence, particularly after an accident put dad out of action.

Not long after going to work for the Riverstone meat company, he fell as he was unloading a side of beef from a company truck. With several fractured discs in his spine he was laid up for months and unable to earn much of a living for the remainder of the year. The company, a part of Lord Vestey's considerable holdings in Australia, gave him nine guineas a week. It was not enough to allay his fears about a future that looked increasingly uncertain. He skimped on luxuries, like a taxi to take him to the hospital, for check-ups. Instead, he limped to the bus stop, leaning on mum, and they laboriously made their way to the hospital at Camperdown, just west of the city. But the medical experts could not seem to agree. One doctor put him in plaster. Another insisted that it had to come off. A third wondered aloud about the effects of heat. Not quite understanding, my mother ironed over his back, persisting a moment too long, so that he was blistered as well.

None too surprisingly he recovered slowly, but when he could walk more or less unaided he bought a milk run with what was left of the savings from Holland. It did not bring in enough, and to make ends meet my mother decided to take the milk truck out in the daytime. She hosed it out, loaded it up with suitcases full of material, and drove to the outskirts of the metropolitan area, sometimes going north, up the tributaries of the Pacific Highway to outlying suburbs where the general store still did as post office and the backroads petered into bush tracks, and sometimes going west to the dusty hills past Parramatta, where you hardly saw so much as a blade of grass, though settlement was so sparse that people selling groceries made the rounds as well. In the land of opportunity she had become a pedlar, like her ancestors.

Her grandfather, Simon Nathans of Arnhem, had peddled drapery, going on foot to farms beyond the city limits, but her father, Marcus, had come up in the world. He used a hand-truck to cart away the iron from the old bridge over the Rhine and sold it for scrap, making enough money to set himself up in business as a meat wholesaler, with a butcher's shop as a sideline.

The butchery was in one of the winding, cobbled lanes of the Nieuwstad, in the centre of Arnhem, where the family lived in a two-room apartment behind the shop. There were four children. My mother, the only girl, was born in 1915. From the age of fourteen she worked in the butchery, as was expected of her, but went to night school to qualify for her escape, and by late

1936 she was a saleswoman in a clothing boutique in Scheveningen, a resort on the North Sea, where she stayed until Bram was mobilized in 1940. The intervening years registered as somehow unreal: with everyone waiting for war she was all the more determined to live it up while she could, and would blow a week's wages on the right hat, or a month's wages on a foalskin coat, before going off for the weekend with her girlfriend, Sonja Sanders, who was so chic, said my mother, that even in Paris people remarked on it.

'What they do in Paris,' mum would tell a housewife from the west of Sydney who had just bought five yards of apricot-coloured nylon in a floral print, 'is drape it here on the shoulder, like this. See how chic . . .' Within the week, or the fortnight, she would drive back to the faded weatherboard cottage in Rooty Hill to collect another fifteen shillings for the fabric the woman was paying off, and stay to admire the cut of her new frock, or to pin up its hem, while the two of them talked about dressmaking.

People responded to her friendliness, but there was an edge of bleak determination behind it. With my father's health still uncertain she failed to tell him, or anyone else, that she disliked the work and so dreaded making the first pitch of the day that she sometimes sat in the truck for half-an-hour, nerving herself up to it.

Once or twice a week she had a stall at the markets. In the school holidays, my brother and I went with her to the market at Wollongong, fifty miles south of Sydney, sprinting off with our sixpences the moment we arrived to have a ride on the donkey down on the beach. If the donkey man shooed us away, we made for the cage of baby chicks dipped in blue dye before running back to ask mum about her customers — we liked to keep track because we got another sixpence when she made a sale.

On our return from Wollongong, late one afternoon in summer, a neighbour stopped by to invite the family to a party. 'Bring the kiddies, too. They can play in the garden. Can't you, dear.' Startled, Jules edged closer to me, keeping his back to the truck. The people from that end of the street seldom spoke to us. Occasionally we caught a glimpse of someone peering from a narrow, upstairs window framed in ivy. They were old people in old houses. No-one played in the gardens, which were dark and forbidding.

'Thank you very much,' I said, because mum had nudged me. She lifted another of the heavy suitcases from the truck. 'Go inside and see if dad's awake.'

'I want to help you,' I said stubbornly, waiting for the woman to go away.

'I was only saying to someone the other day that you Dutch people work so hard.'

'Not really . . .'

'Well, there's another invitation for Boxing Day,' mum said later, while we were finishing dinner, 'from that woman with the beautiful grey hair, the colour of the Wynberg's Holden.'

'The Wynberg's Holden is blue.'

'I didn't know you were so interested in hair styles, Paul.'

'We had two rides on the donkey,' I told my cousin, who usually came with us, 'and a picnic.'

'We had fish and chips,' said Jules. We spoke to each other in Dutch-accented English and to our parents, by then, in English-accented Dutch.

'I always take them to that place near the Cook's River because it makes me think of the Rhine. It's lovely there.'

'There's no comparison with the northern suburbs. You've said so yourself.' Uncle Bram's tone did not allow any argument.

'I don't feel at all nostalgic,' said my aunt, who had adapted to life in Sydney with apparent ease. Quieter than the others, she seemed to retreat into herself if they reminisced. 'For me, it's a closed chapter. I'd rather look ahead.'

My mother turned the meaning of a word around if it got in her way. 'I'm not nostalgic either,' she paused, and tapped a couple of Senior Service from the pack, 'but I like to be reminded of some things and, in any case, we should give the children an idea of how it was.' It sounded impressive and she looked around as if daring anyone to disagree.

'She's quite right.' With an unlit cigarette in the side of his mouth, dad walked around the table, fumbled for matches — feeling in every pocket before he found them on top of the fridge — and with the usual series of flourishes, he lit her cigarette.

'Only today I was telling them how we used to swim all day — from morning to night — in the swimming baths on the Rhine . . .'

'Your mother has a good imagination.'

'Leave my little sister alone,' Uncle Nick bellowed in Dutch as he clumped through the back door, into the kitchen, as if he were on his own, though his wife was right behind him. Three people spoke at once. The benches scraped on the linoleum as we shifted along to make room for Nick, who filled any room to bursting.

'The lantana's looking good,' he shouted exuberantly, 'I don't know how you do it.' My mother had carefully planted lantana all the way along the back fence, unaware that it was a despised weed until she showed the flame-coloured flowers to one of our neighbours.

'You should be on stage, Nico. Let some other people share in the pleasure.'

'Why don't they go inside?' Ali was clearing the table, reaching across the men, who did not budge.

'That big white house halfway down the street, is that where the bank manager lives?'

'What would you know about it?'

'Calm down, Paul.'

'A pipsqueak of a fellow in such a big house,' mused Uncle Nick. 'He said good evening, but I could tell he didn't mean it.'

In the bank manager's eyes, we were lowering the tone of the neighbourhood. Exasperated about the trucks and battered vans parked along Lewis Street on Sundays, when countless people called on us, he had asked dad if he knew anyone at all who drove an ordinary sedan.

'Oh well,' said mum, 'if you threw salt on every snail, you'd be busy all day long. People can think what they want. I couldn't be bothered finding a meaning behind every word.'

'Is anyone making coffee?' said Uncle Bram sternly.

Family occasions like that followed something of a pattern. The ritual was to be much the same, from month to month, and year to year, long after they had arrived in Sydney. Doubtless it reminded them of home.

There is a Dutch word 'gezellig' which recurs again and again in everyday conversation, as a refrain that hints at the superior domestic habits of those fortunate enough to have been born in Holland. It does not translate at all well. The English words 'cosy' and 'convivial' do not begin to suggest the infinite variations on the theme, but in its purest form, 'gezelligheid' demands the company of intimates, enough food for a garrison and an atmosphere most unlike the atmosphere suggested by Van Gogh's painting of the silent, grim-faced 'Potato Eaters'.

Our clan specialized in gezelligheid, even after we had stopped living on top of each other. The aunts and uncles trooped in at least once a week, probably protesting that they wanted nothing but a 'kopje koffie'. This overture was strictly rhetorical. While setting the coffee table with home-made Dutch buttercake, miniature chocolate éclairs, a dish of bon bons and the coffee-pot, my mother would explain that she had not had the time to stock up.

People were respectfully silent for an instant, as the coffee was poured, and then having smiled with satisfaction at the buttercake — though he had not yet helped himself to the largest slice — Uncle Nick would lean back luxuriantly, saying, 'ah, gezellig'.

'Ja, gezellig,' someone would immediately agree. If my brother and I were in the room, there would be a short pause, and a meaningful look from mum, until one of us vigorously assented: 'Ja, echt gezellig . . .',

But gezelligheid depended as much on the atmosphere as on the food, and a meal in a restaurant in Sydney never came up to expectation. In Holland, the tiniest ginmill is chock-a-block with ornamental pewter and copper. Persian rugs are laid on the tables and potted geraniums are set in the windowsills. The very sight is enough to make an expatriate exclaim: '. . . ah, echt gezellig', and what she means is that it looks like home.

Though outwardly eager to assimilate as soon as possible, the Dutch maintained the appurtenances of 'home' when they went abroad. We had left most of the furniture behind, but had brought along a few bits and pieces; enough, so it seemed, to compose the picture my mother must have carried in her mind, and she would glance about the living room as if taking stock, her eyes drifting from the copper kettle on the pristine hearth to the samovar beside the bowl of fruit on the rosewood side-board, before she asserted in Dutch, to no-one in particular: 'Say what you like but I find this echt gezellig . . .'

In private, we congratulated ourselves on our own good taste, as if the same, perfectly ordinary sofa, installed next door, could not possibly have created quite the effect. Not that my parents spelled it out with such precision. No sooner had they come to Australia than they picked up the habit expected of immigrants, and loudly sang the praises of the local way of life; but there was a subtext, suggested with every repetition of the word gezellig, and it told us that we had a certain flair: we knew how to live well.

TWO
Australian Gothic

Without Mr McCarthy's assistance, we could never have passed ourselves off as natives. Mr McCarthy, who was a legend in Manly, taught us how to swim. For going on a century, he had been a fixture on the boardwalk at the deep end of the harbour pool. He wore a baggy one-piece swimsuit and seemed to have no use at all for passing fads or fashionable equipment.

Instead, with a few brisk words of reassurance, he tied an antique yellowing canvas contraption around my middle and grasped his end of the rope. It was a long way down the ladder. I dug in, towards the end, and found myself dangling in the air for an instant before I was lowered into the water. Mr McCarthy towed me along, rasping out instructions from high up on the boardwalk. It looked as if he had not got his feet wet in fifty years.

The boys weren't impressed to hear that I could swim. Jules, who was five years old, clung to the railings at the back of the pool as if nothing could prise him loose, but it was Cousin Ron's turn to be done up in the vintage float. His teeth were chattering and his face was white against his carroty-coloured hair. 'Come on, Bluey,' said Mr McCarthy, 'we haven't got all day.'

It was our formal introduction to Manly, the capital of the district. Manly was as improbable as a child's drawing of a sea-side resort. Palm trees were planted in the middle of The Corso, the main street across the spit of land between the harbour and the ocean. Lorikeets fluttered in the Norfolk pines along the seashore, deserted midweek and crowded of a Sunday, when hundreds of striped deckchairs were set out in rows on the crazy-paving of the promenade at the south end of the beach.

Manly might have existed in another realm. It was as particular as a toy world, with its own sun shining on its own sea, even if the tin sign in sight of the ferry terminal said Manly was seven miles from Sydney . . . 'seven miles from Sydney *and* a thousand miles from care'. The people who arrived by ferry for the day were from the western side of the city, from suburbs with names that hung in the air for a moment and blew away again, like dust on a dry street, as if the region that they inhabited was just a dirty blur on the way to somewhere else. They came and went and came and went without impinging on Manly's imperturbable sense of its own completeness.

From our perspective, Manly appeared in any number of guises, because it was where we went for the niceties, the optional extras my mother translated into rites de passage. From the age of eight, I studied ballet at Miss Grant's in Manly, and since my mother worked by then at a dress shop around the corner, I was parked at the ballet school every Saturday, from nine until after twelve. The trade-offs were not spelled out, but Miss Grant, a small, voluble woman with a mass of dark hair, was still getting a discount on her XSSW dresses more than a decade after I had turned in my toe-shoes.

If there was a quiet moment in the studio, I was a captive audience for the pianist, who talked of nothing but her daughter, Fiona, a fat, freckled girl widely thought to have the native ability of Moira Shearer. At the ballet school's concert, a local institution, Fiona had nine starring roles and I appeared, briefly, at the tail end of a chorus line in the grand finale.

The photograph of the occasion would give a paedophile goose pimples. The girls are in short, pleated skirts and sailor tops, and the little ones at the front have assured theatrical smiles although they are kneeling in an uncomfortable position.

I am at the end of the front row. My lipstick has worn off, my sailor cap has fallen off and the whites of my eyes are showing. No other child seems quite so oblivious to the conventions of a group photograph, and it is evident that I am lost in the moment, intent only on keeping one knee at right angles to the other and my toes nicely turned out.

We stayed on stage when the pictures had been taken and people from the audience came up, one or two at a time, with bouquets of gladioli swathed in cellophane. I held my breath, wondering if anyone had mentioned this lovely tradition to my mother. 'Everybody gets them,' whispered Fiona's understudy. A bunch of flowers had come adrift. The air smelled of gardenia and one of the cygnets from *Swan Lake* kept sneezing. People were starting to leave by the time that I saw my mother, halfway down the aisle, but I could not make out what she was carrying until she reached up to hand it to the dancing teacher.

'Isn't it sweet,' said Miss Grant, holding out a small Dutch clog with a cactus growing in it. I burst into tears backstage and it was quite a while before mum went so far as to rescue the pot plant that I had dumped on the floor.

On my tenth birthday, we moved to a house in Harbord, two miles up the coast from Manly. The double-fronted red brick bungalow was at the end of a short street that ran into about five acres of bush. Proud at having conjured up a house of our very own, we had an unveiling ceremony with a towel draped over wrought-iron letters that spelled out 'Chardonne', the name of the village in Switzerland where mum and dad were married. It was agreed again and again that the house was sumptuous, with a bedroom for each of us kids and French doors leading to the terraces at the front and the back.

Within a day or two, the children from next door had ventured into our living room, to play marbles on the reddish carpet my parents had bought in Karachi, and they looked around in amazement. Their place was dark as a dungeon and they must have thought ours to be exposed to the elements, because the room was full of light and the French doors were usually open.

Unlike the neighbours, we frequently ate alfresco. Mrs Turner, the lady next door, said it was very Continental, and since we were so casual about what belonged inside and outside, she felt free to wander over for a natter if she saw us setting the table on the terrace. The potatoes burned while she complained in an intense whisper about Mr T., a quiet, moon-faced, harmless looking man who was always fixing things around the yard. My mother, who was a little uncomfortable in the confessor's role, did not want to set the parameters of the friendship. The Turners had made us welcome from the first. Mrs T. said that she had always liked Dutch people, though she did not seem to know any others. In fact the details of our ancestry did not mean much out our way, high on a headland between two beaches, a thousand and two miles from care.

Insular or not, the locals had a peninsular mentality, an illusory sense of security that history couldn't touch. Though my brother and I came across the rusted metal rings and concrete remains of an old gun emplacement, on the rocks at North Curl Curl, it was impossible to imagine anyone anticipating enemy action on Curl Curl beach, a mile-long stretch of sand we might have all to ourselves on a grey day after Stewart House closed for the winter.

Stewart House, across the beach from the surf club, was a holiday home for children from the outback whose lives were so cursed that they had never been to the beach before. If the teachers at the primary school in Harbord wanted to remind us of our advantages, they talked about the poor kiddies at Stewart House, managing to suggest that we could fix everything for those less fortunate than ourselves if only we organized enough fetes and raffles. No-one questioned the importance of the cause — when it came to our spectacular stretch of coast, we had a sense of noblesse oblige.

The neighbourhood my family moved to in 1956 was lower

middle-class. Our deadend street was at the frontier of development, with a couple of vacant lots between the Turner's place and the cottage on the corner. Across from the few houses was the rocky inside slope of the cliff, with nothing but the surveyor's pegs to mark it, officially, as the other side of the street. Five or six children came exploring with Tom Turner, my brother and me to make cubbies in the cool, sandstone caves, after cleaning out the crushed-up Ardath packets and the Frenchies. We played at being Captain Silver of the Seahound, the hero of a radio serial, or we dressed as Red Indians, near-enough, with a feather stuck in a headband, and wriggled along the ground to hide out in damp little gullies overgrown with wildflowers.

Our territory, which was just large enough to be mysterious, was spoiled in the end. Split-level homes now cling to what is left of the cliff face and home units are wedged wall-to-wall on the few acres beyond our old place, but at the time, settlement was sparse enough for us to identify the neighbourhood characters.

People who arrived in the 'fifties built in brick, a sign of steadfast respectability, but around the corner, along Wyndora Avenue, were several weatherboard cottages inhabited by aging widows with decrepit dogs, and even the dogs slunk by, on the opposite side of the street, when they passed the local source of shame, an ancient fibro shack we dismissed as little better than a lean-to. It stood in a large yard of mangy grass littered with worn-out Kelvinators and the hulks of motorcycles cannibalized for spare parts. The front door was always open, or off its hinges. The rickety porch, raised a few inches from the ground, was furnished with a sprung sofa that usually had someone in motorcyle boots lounging on it.

A gang of boys old enough to be delinquents but too young to leave home hung around the yard at all hours of the day and night. They had yellow hair, wore oil-stained overalls and, according to my mother, looked hungry. There was a sister,

Elaine, a poor, dim thing my age who was always missing school and never in the company of another girl, at home. No-one knew about their parents so we were forced to invent a father who drank. The boys kept three or four scrawny blue cattle dogs which launched themselves, snarling, at any living thing, but were pulled up short when they ran out of chain. You could not help feeling sorry for the dogs, but Mrs Turner said the boys were bludgers, a word I associated with lounging about on an outdoor sofa.

They never took a bit of notice of the neighbours, but we were wary going past their place, perhaps because it did not fit. It was the slovenly sort of property you saw on the outskirts of country towns, or the side roads past Liverpool, west of Sydney, where suburbia petered out; and its inhabitants seemed to exist on the margins of society, in isolation. They looked like people relating only accidentally to one another. It was evident that they had managed to escape all the constraints and comforts of our family life: they got away with acting like orphans in their dirty overalls. I thought of them as genuine Australians.

By the time I was eleven or twelve years old, I was aware that something was missing from the domestic arrangements that the locals made, but I was intrigued by the way that they lived, and going next door to watch television had some of the enchantment of a long journey. In the Turner's house the rooms were small, the windows were small and papery Holland blinds the colour of parchment were drawn at all times in all seasons.

The furniture to be made out in the crepuscular gloom of the living room was in a patterned plush with the nap worn off. One of the pictures on the walls was a print of a dark-skinned woman with a turban on her head. I forget the others. There were no books. The glass vase on the mantelpiece was always empty. The room had a heaviness, as if nothing would ever change, but with the arrival of the television set, soon after television was introduced, the chairs had been lined up on either side of the sofa, so everyone could sit in the front stalls, on the one or two days a year that the Turners were together in the same room. Usually, of an evening, Mrs T. did not leave the kitchen and her husband was hardly to be seen at all. If the two of them were at war they did not speak to each other, and although this called for a degree of self-restraint unimaginable in our household, they hardly seemed to notice it as anything out of the ordinary, because Jules and I might be invited to stay, regardless of the conflict.

Tom Turner, a wiry, freckled boy about my brother's age, ran messages from one parent to the other, drifting out the back to shout, 'Mum says tea's ready'. The neighbours' tea seemed to be the only thing they had agreed on when they were married. It was a mixed grill with a pork sausage, a small lamb chop, a rasher of bacon, half a grilled tomato, a puddle of peas and a scoop of mashed potato. The unchanging nature of the meal never failed to surprise me; nor did the occasion itself, because Tom Turner and his little sister were left to their own devices at dinner and, in spite of the arrangement of the furniture, we sat cross-legged on the living room floor, with our plates in our laps, the lights switched off and the telly turned up loud. In our house, in contrast, the only excuse for being left alone was that you had homework, or a headache, conversations went on uninterrupted between two rooms and everyone had to report in for meals, around the kitchen table.

We were drawn to the kitchen, in any case, but it was difficult to imagine that happening in an Australian household, judging by the people that I visited after school. The kitchens were most unfamiliar. If there was any food, it was hidden away in high cupboards: biscuit tins were out of reach; instead of fruit there were wax bananas on a cut-glass epergne, and the cannisters in mint condition had obviously been squared away with a ruler.

The mothers of some of my friends at school played tennis, three times a week, and I could see them at Curl Curl Tennis Club, in those little white frocks and frilly pants, having afternoon tea with an urn and sponge fingers. When you visited, they seemed to be full-up with the tennis club sponge and the devon sandwiches cut in doll-sized triangles, because they hardly ever asked if you wanted something to eat, if they even went so far as to appear in the kitchen while we were out getting the lime cordial. I thought they were unnatural. In public, parents and children acted as if they hardly knew each other and they weren't much different in private. If they kissed at all, they kissed like people worried about giving each other 'flu. It did not surprise me that my pals couldn't wait to get away from home, but I, for the most part, could not wait to get away from school.

The first day at Harbord Primary had started with a misunderstanding. Mrs Kelsick, the fourth-class teacher, had made a speech. The general drift of it was that I was a New Girl who had only just got to lovely Australia. 'Of course we'll do our best to make her feel at home, won't we girls,' she said. Occupied in trying not to take the giggling at the back of the room personally, I waited to correct her until the others had gone out for playlunch. 'Yes, dear,' she said patiently, 'of course you feel at home here.'

The first impression died hard. Although I spoke in a broad Australian accent at school, Mrs Kelsick remained convinced that I was just off the boat, and if she marvelled over my spelling the class was reminded that it was being shown up by a New Australian. I would vow to lose the spelling bee next time but I couldn't help myself, and Mrs Kelsick did not seem to know, as yet, that ex-wogs were always the best spellers, something I had found out at the primary school in Balgowlah Heights, where Jules, Ron and I took line honours until a skinny kid from Yugoslavia turned up and got 'aquarium' right the first time.

But you could not have accused the people who taught in the girls' school at Harbord Primary of laying too much stress on academic accomplishment. Our fifth-class teacher, Mrs G., who wore black jumpers and jangling jewellery, considered it banal to give lessons in reading, writing and arithmetic, and did so only rarely. Determinedly unaware of what was going on in the rest of the school, she seemed astonished to hear that we were not allowed to use biros, which were supposed to muck up our handwriting, and she picked up a regulation school pen with a loose, inky nib as if it were a bit of mummified stuff dug up from a smelly old tomb.

Almost any reminder of ordinary academic life prompted her to rhapsodize about the potential of the human spirit, in a long, flowery speech that no-one in the class understood. But it was clear that Mrs G. disapproved of everything we thought we were at school for, and we spent a year relaxing with a teacher ahead of her time, who was encouraging us to be 'creative'. Being creative involved a less than demanding agenda in which we spent an entire term in preparation for a pageant at the Conservatorium, not only rehearsing but doing classes in something Mrs G. called 'movement', which seemed to mean wriggling like a snake and stalking like a tiger, though we usually lay around giggling demonically, covered in dust and soaked in sweat. 'Horses sweat,' said Mrs G. in her one reflexive remark we were to hear from other teachers, 'men perspire, ladies glow . . .'

No-one paid particular attention to our school's performance at the pageant and the wind must have gone out of Mrs G.'s sails, because she drooped around for a bit before deciding to bring a pet, one of a pair of toothless terriers, to school. It sat in its basket yapping at her while we did classes in basketball, but the arrangement did not last long, because Mrs G. suddenly disappeared.

Her absence went unexplained and we decided that it was the terrier's fault, because the headmistress's pet, Poochy, a fat, drooling blue cattle dog, was supposed to have the run of the place. The headmistress fed him biscuits in Assembly and Poochy had followed her everywhere until he started stalking the terrier. The gentle, young teacher who took over our class for a bit had barely got us accustomed to sitting behind a desk again when the holidays started.

Indeed about half the class did so badly in the final examinations the following year that they were sent to the home science high school at Manly where girls were taught to cook, to type and to keep ledgers, in case they had to help their husbands with the books when they grew up. The rest of us were supposed to go to Manly Girls' High, a school so new that construction had not been completed in time for our arrival. Instead, we were dispatched to the boy's school at Narrabeen, about seven miles further out along the northern beaches, a bureaucratic sleight-of-hand which may have caused some confusion. Though in different classes from the boys, we weren't allowed to forget that we were on their turf, and the photograph of my first-year class shows forty-something girls posed near a sign saying 'Narrabeen Boys' High School'. In my case, however, another confusion of identity had been cleared up — in the course of the year I became an official Australian.

No-one in my family was inclined to over-anticipate events and several things went awry at the naturalization ceremony at Brookvale Town Hall. The Italian children being naturalized were dressed in their Sunday best, frilled-up from head to toe, but my brother and I looked like pathetic immigrants in our school uniforms, and our irritation was nothing compared to mum's. It was only after the ceremony had started that she realized that she was supposed to foreswear allegiance to the Dutch queen, Wilhemina of misty memory, and she was so cross about it that we had to persuade her not to tell off the mayor, there and then. Views were exchanged in intense whispers, and though dad seemed to think we might be deported if we drew attention to ourselves, mum — who looked to be on the verge of tears, which was unlike her — said that she didn't care one bit.

My mother loved Queen Wilhemina, frequently spoke of her as if she used to drop in for a kopje koffie, and claimed without batting an eyelash that Wilhemina had got about on a bicycle, unescorted, during the war, to cheer up the masses. Indeed, I was to feel almost betrayed by the queen when I discovered, a bit belatedly, that she had spent the war years in England.

Wilhemina may have counted as a family friend, but as a rule neither my brother nor I cared much for royalty. Uprootedness made us republicans, early on, especially after we had gone through the rigmarole at the primary school in Balgowlah Heights, where everyone lined up in the playground, ten minutes before the bell for the first lesson, to sing 'God Save the King' as a teacher's pet pulled at the rope that raised the flag. Incapable of resisting a chance to clown around, I had been dragged out in front of the school at the age of seven by the headmaster, Mr Piper, because I had saluted with both arms at once. He insisted on an explanation. Red-faced at the best of times, he went a dangerous colour when I whispered that I had only done it for a joke. I was kept in for hours, saluted the king from the sidelines for a week, and never got into Mr Piper's good books again.

It did not make me feel more respectful, the following year, when we were among the thousands of school children included in the staging of Queen Elizabeth's coronation tour, because we were at the cricket ground three and a half hours before she whisked past in an open jeep, with a cranky look on her face instead of the usual frozen smile. Nor were my parents impressed by all the pomp and pageantry. I suppose they had seen enough of it in Europe. Though Queen Elizabeth had gone to David Jones, our favourite store, for a banquet, dressed in a yellow tulle frock embroidered with wattle, it was not enough to redeem her in my family's eyes: mum said that a proper queen, like Juliana could remember speeches instead of reading them, and that was more or less the last word on Queen Elizabeth in our household until we owed her allegiance and considered refusing to honour the debt.

THREE
The Playing Fields of Manly

The students at Manly Girls' High had the status of unwelcome visitors, like people who come in tourist buses and leave nothing but litter behind. In fact, we were pioneers. It was up to us to scuff the parquet outside the principal's office and to deface the toilets with graffiti, even if the cubicle with the sanitary napkin disposal unit was untouched, because no-one wanted to be seen going into it. We had no older girls to guide us and, like the First Settlers, no credible traditions except those that we invented, like stealing the cabbages from the Chinese market garden beyond the boundary at the back of the school.

But while we were intent on forging our own heritage, the principal had very different ideas about it. Miss Knodler, the headmistress of Manly Girls', was a traditionalist: to her way of thinking, individual circumstances did not excuse any girl from fitting in with a formula that should have been universal, and she frequently lectured us about it. 'When we speak of Christian Behaviour or British Democracy or the Australian Way of Life, we all know what is meant,' she assured us, by way of a welcome. 'They are a tradition. The playing fields of Eton have been written into history . . .'

The allusion to Eton was fanciful, to say the least, and from the first, we failed to live up to Miss Knodler's expectations. The headmistress was a small, unforgiving, fastidious woman in her fifties who reacted to our collective lack of class with unconcealed distaste. She suggested that we try to sound well-bred, by speaking, as she put it, with a 'naice exsent' and, that said, she would revert to the vexing question of our appearance. The school uniform included such essentials as dark-brown gloves in winter, and a panama hat in summer, but none got as much airtime as the regulation beige socks, because the rebels insisted on wearing white socks instead. They claimed, not completely convincingly, that their parents could not afford to buy extra socks as well as shirts and ties and blazer and green gym bloomers.

'I've told you, gels, soak them in tea,' Miss Knodler said between clenched teeth in Assembly. Occasionally she worked herself up until she was beyond speech, and just stood there, shivering with rage. It was a terrifying sight. A stroke had left one side of her face partially paralyzed and one of her hands convulsively curled. But it was impossible to feel a twinge of compassion for her condition: the relationship was too unequal.

Briskly assessed and found wanting, students at Manly Girls' High were punished, en masse, by being treated like intruders. More than half the school grounds were out of bounds because we were not allowed anywhere near Miss Knodler's garden, out the front. Crossing the lobby in front of her office meant an afternoon's detention, if you were lucky. The Education Department's standard set of prints hung in the lobby. To this day, I associate the picture of God stretching out his finger to Adam with the beckoning claw of the principal when you had been summoned to her office.

In one encyclical published in the school magazine, Miss Knodler wondered aloud about our image. 'When people think of this school, what will they associate with us?' Her answer predictably put the property first. '. . . the beautiful modern building . . . the equally beautiful grounds'. From her perspective, we gels infested a brand-new school, albeit a series of cement and glass boxes on concrete poured over a geographical no-man's land.

Our school was separated from the boys' high school at the

bottom of the hill by a swamp, a corner of Curl Curl Dump and what was left of the Chinese market garden. We were participating in the suburban sprawl of the 'sixties. Across the street, Harbord's small brick cottages petered into unkempt Brookvale, an area zoned to allow light industry. Surfboard-makers were setting up shop towards the bottom of the hill, where reckless Manly Girls paused to talk to feckless surfies.

Gordonstoun, another school Miss Knodler mentioned in dispatches, was getting Prince Charles, but our real heros were closer to hand. Manly Girls was close to a number of beaches. Long before the tabloids noticed that surfing was 'a new cult of juvenile behaviour', most of the girls I knew were camped out on Freshwater throughout the summer. Poor Miss Knodler, fantasizing about Edwardian tradition, was condemned to a school quickly known for the number of its nymphets who pranced half-naked around the northern beaches.

My friends at school regarded themselves as part of the Freshwater fraternity. The other girls who hung around with surfies did domestic science and were sexually knowing, but my clique thought of adolescence in much the way that some Indian tribes in the Amazon think of the road being driven through the bush. It was taking us where we were not sure we wanted to go.

Something of the style of our group had been determined in primary school by its ringleader Helen Scott, who looked like a china doll but had the instinctive imperiousness of a Prussian cavalry commander. I met her when we were ten years old. At the time, Helen was endowed with a cricket bat and an uncanny hold over her acolytes, who vied to buy her Panda chips and Pepsi, with their Oslo-lunch money. She was golden-haired, tiny, and so physically unformed that the others in the gang were even more revolted than is usual by their developing bodies. The start of menstruation was not just a sudden stain on one's knickers, but a lasting stigma. Not long ago, I mentioned a mutual acquaintance to someone from the old gang at school. 'Oh, I remember her,' said the woman, who by then had teenage children of her own, 'she got her periods in sixth class.'

At the age of twelve none of us could bring ourselves to say 'brassiere' or even 'bra'. Instead we mumbled 'over-the-shoulder-boulder-holder', one of a series of euphemisms that hinted at our agitation about the female form and its official functions. Those who joined the gang in high school were also tomboys, unwilling to give in to the feeling of sluggishness that anticipates adolescence. In first year at high school, girls who would later be noted for their decorum clung together, like survivors of a shipwreck marooned among primitives, and we played ballgames with the boys, insisting on being taken as equals — not because we were liberated before our time, but because we did not like the idea of being girls.

Our inchoate sexuality also troubled the overseers at Manly Girls'. Even our restlessness was a threat, and time and time again we were ordered to walk, not to run, in the school corridors. Miss Knodler, whose favourite adjective was 'seemly', threatened more than once to punish the girls she had seen sprinting to or from school. She said that it was a disgraceful sight.

It was about what we expected of Miss Knodler, but a couple of our teachers were at least as prudish. They were set off-course when the domestic realities intruded on the formal nicety of a text, but few reacted quite as viscerally as the English Mistress, Mrs Davis, who censored a play a girl wrote in class because it had a reference to false teeth. I was to see another side of her querulousness. In a fourth-year essay on *Mr Polly*, I wrote that Mr P. and his wife were 'incompatible', and having handed it in, waited in vain to be complimented on my cleverness. But Mrs Davis had slashed out the word 'incompatible' as if it were an indecency. Still sure of myself I queried her. I swear she blushed. It was inappropriate, she said, and turned away.

Our teachers lived according to their own rules, and that could mean that real desperation went unnoticed. Mr A., who taught biology, went so far as to kill himself, though he waited, considerately, until the school holidays. Senior students who heard about it felt guilty, remembering that they had plagued poor Mr A. for explanations, after noticing that he got a bit sweaty when discussing the ramifications of the reproductive cycle in the stickleback.

Of course there were teachers prepared to deal with the only questions to which we wanted answers. My biology teacher, Lynn Hall, a progressive just out of teachers' college, gave us in third year so coolly precise an account of the sexual act that the class was scandalized into silence, before a couple of girls nerved themselves up to ask (a) did it hurt? (b) did you have to get pregnant and (c) what happened if people, um, you know, before they got married?

The trouble with Miss Hall's clear-headed explanation was that it did not relate to the few facts one had picked up, which were that sex was (a) dirty, (b) furtive and (c) inexplicable. The very last thing that would have occurred to us as teenagers was that love-making was normal. If we spoke about it at lunchtime, when the gang commandeered one of the few bits of grass for miles around that Miss Knodler had not declared out-of-bounds, we spoke as if it had nothing to do with us. The public consensus was that only sluts went all the way. The official sexual code of the surfing world, circa 1962, followed age-old rules. Public perception was everything: a girl who was not a virgin had the makings of a gangbang, and someone who changed boyfriends a little too soon might be condemned for all time. The girls I knew portrayed themselves as novices, understandably enough, taking part in conversations in which we wondered aloud, for instance, if humans did It 'like dogs' or if It left a mark. For a while, we promoted the theory that sex-crazed girls could be identified by the hollow between their thighs.

Everyone was prevaricating at some level, of course, but it was not all play-acting. I, for one, was wilfully naive. It was beyond me to assemble such information as I had into a coherent picture. In fact, I was to remember myself at the age of sixteen as even more innocent than I was, as if to suggest that I had been ashamed of inexpressible, inadmissable longings, and suppressed the recollection.

None of it was aired in any meaningful way. Instead, at lunchtime, sprawled on the grass sunbaking, with our skirts hiked up and our heads resting on each other's stomachs, we usually talked about boys. Without a boyfriend, or a prospect, there was not much to say. The conversations did not range wide, and the character of the boys who tramped through so many of the stories was often left to the imagination. But names were waved like flags. Hair? Eyes? Height? We might have been stamping their passports. These details sketched in, a girl would say where she had been on Saturday night, waiting for the chorus of sighs when she got to the bit about sitting in the ute, 'talking'. The surf, two miles off, thrummed through every story. Half the skinny girls in the gang hankered after boys who could hang five, and grew thinner still, pining for the day that they, too, could be left in the car parked outside the Newport Arms, while Mr Right went off to drink with his mates. Meanwhile, they were marking time at the Church of England Fellowship, which was said to have better boys than the Presbyterian organization.

In short, the girls in our gang wavered between sin and salvation. The out-and-out tarts with peroxided hair in the cooking classes knew which side they were on, and their sins carried the weight of commitment, but a few of my friends caught more heat from the headmistress. Those re-elected as prefects year after year included Helen Scott, whose growing rebelliousness failed to affect her following. By the time that she was in fourth year, Helen was a regular at Dee Why beach, the acropolis of the surfing scene, where she wore what must have been the smallest bikini in Warringah Shire. A teacher from the boys' school who was at the beach, spying on his off-duty prefects, mentioned it to our headmistress. From that moment on, Helen was a symptom of Miss Knodler's frustrated ambition. The interrogation did not go well. Infuriated by the gel's insolently cool demeanour, Miss Knodler flipped her lid, seized her, and bashed her head against the wall until a secretary intervened.

I was unable to make such an impression on Miss Knodler, whose final-year reference (a convention she could not avoid), was a testimonial to the tepid endorsement. Something of an expert in damning with faint praise, she had summed up most of my school reports as 'mainly satisfactory'. In the reference she outdid herself, noting only that I had 'a definite personality with independent ideas' and was 'honest, obliging and cheerful'.

Miss Knodler may have been unaware of the one sphere of school life in which I excelled. I had invented it out of necessity: I had nothing else going for me. With the exception of a couple of troublemakers — outsiders, like myself — the other girls in the gang were slender, athletic and agreeable. They had admirers in the junior years, they did not strive for effect, and they were perfectly adapted to the only things which mattered in our school.

I did not have a following, but once a year, on my birthday, I would pretend that I was popular. My mother turned it into an extravaganza, staging what we thought of as an immensely classy party. Bristling with self-importance, I would pass out invitations to a dozen girls, meanwhile urging a conspiratorial silence which was supposed to remind them that another battalion of my best friends was being excluded.

My mother usually took us to the pictures in the city, but the best bit came later when we re-assembled at home for the birthday dinner. The pièce de résistance was Bombe Alaska. No-one else had Bombe Alaska for a birthday. No other mother went to so much trouble. Girls who usually had to content themselves with sausage rolls and spongecake sometimes mentioned our Bombe Alaska, months later. Though the fuss and fanfare associated with my birthday were irresistible, I wondered in private if we were overdoing it: I did not want to hurt mum's feelings, but I knew that a real Australian would not try so hard.

Not that I expected to be mistaken for a native, for as I say, the natives I knew well were golden-skinned, lithe and blonde. I had hair like faded serge, thighs which made gym teachers redouble their efforts and so few male admirers (i.e. none) that I practised flirting with my brother's friend, Porky. I fluttered my eyelashes at Porky who asked, solicitously, if there was something wrong with my eyes, and that was that. Unable to make the grade as an Australian, I became the cultivated Continental. Out our way, there was little competition in this league, and the props were right to hand.

No-one ever got so much mileage out of pumpernickel, stinky cheese and cold Wiener Schnitzels. Girls who hardly deigned to talk to me could not keep their eyes off my doorstep sandwiches, goggling beforehand at the very sight of the recycled paper bags, blotched with grease from the schnitzels. They had lookalike paper bags, with two neat twirls at the top, and lookalike lunches. I never could understand the wogs who begged their mothers to make them lunches like that, little white triangles of bread patted with peanut butter. Why would anyone give up a moment of glory?

To prolong it, I resorted to another stratagem, reinforcing my own pretensions to intellectual sophistication by re-inventing my family. The way I talked about them suggested that my dad, the peasant, dipped into Schopenhauer for a pick-me-up, while mum gossiped to us about the antiphonies in Gabrieli. In fact, we subscribed to *Readers' Digest*, had never heard of *Nation*, and thought of Tchaikowsky's 'Nutcracker Suite' as the high point of musical history. We respected Art, but we did not know much about it.

My father fell asleep with the bedlamp on, reading and rereading chapter two of the latest Herman Wouk, and mum said that *The Grapes of Wrath* was heavy-going. Literature was my department. Condemned to mope around the house most afternoons, I stuck my nose in a book, and signalled my personal acquaintance with the avant-garde by being first off the starting blocks with *Catcher in the Rye*.

I told the others about it at lunchtime while we were swapping sandwiches, a ritual which ended in an exchange of pleasantries. Someone would make a polite comment about immigrants, and then there was murmured agreement that Australia was lucky to have its foreigners. Elsewhere there may have been people applauding the Europeans who turned up for concerts at the Sydney Town Hall, but Continental culture had had a more specific impact, in our district, and the gang was grateful. It was noted, almost from day to day, that the immigrants had brought salami to Australia. I took it as a compliment, but now that I think back on it, I realize that no-one else in the gang produced salami sandwiches. I suppose that it was the concept of salami, not the taste, that pleased them.

If there was a negative aspect to immigration, it was not discussed in my hearing, except, perhaps, for the time that I flopped down next to a girl called Gibbs in art class, and she made a face as if she were going to be sick. 'What's wrong?' I said. Gibbs kept her hand over her mouth, but she did not beat around the bush. 'You smell funny,' she said, 'you smell of, uh, garlic . . .' She flat-out refused to believe that we never had garlic at home, not even in the salami, and I was forced to conclude that my presence reminded her of the stuff, as if to say that it was the concept of garlic which had got up her nostril.

But in the usual course of things, I was encouraged to play the Continental. 'It's so tasteful at your house,' girls said, adopting my own view of the matter, before they mentioned our Rosenthal china, or the cognac that Helen Scott and I had burned off in an unsuccessful experiment with espresso coffee. These accoutrements had lodged in the minds of my friends at school, and come to represent all that they wanted to know about Europe. I had got away with it.

FOUR
The War

Not long ago, someone who took us under his wing when we moved to Lewis Street, Balgowlah, told my mother he hadn't known that we were Jewish. 'How is it possible?' she asked him, as if he had wilfully refused to acknowledge the obvious. It wasn't the sort of thing you had to tell the neighbours, in Europe, and my guess is that she never really understood what it meant to have settled in a part of Sydney where Jews existed only in theory. Things may have been different in Coogee, in the eastern suburbs, where whole streets suddenly seemed to fill with what the *Bulletin* called 'the brooding aliens' from the DP camps, and the kindest local interpretation was that a Jew was a generic reffo, lost property without a rightful destination. Out our way, though, there was no reason to associate my mother's determined gaiety with what was, strictly speaking, a figure of speech: even if Jews crept in the conversational back door as pawnbrokers or people who stiffed you in a financial transaction, why would they suddenly materialize out of thin air to park those bloody trucks and vans across the street?

Even someone who knew a thing or two about the Jews could have been confused by our behaviour, particularly at Christmas, which we overdid a bit the first time around, delivering more presents than the Smith Family, too excited to notice the embarrassed pause before someone's mum told us to come back later because they still had to wrap the gifts for us. The only way we could possibly have drawn attention to ourselves was in our eagerness to conform, but my mother appears to have forgotten the degree of her discretion in those days, when we were trying to fit in without people making too much of a fuss.

By no means all the Jews who fled from Europe were in a hurry to flaunt the pedigree. Sydney seemed to be a haven, but who could be sure? The Jews of Amsterdam had felt more or less secure for centuries and, in the years before the war, were inclined to brag about their assimilation, going so far as to contrast it with the 'primitive' way of life in the shtetls of Eastern Europe.

It made very little difference, in the end. More than three-quarters of the Jews in Holland were murdered by the Nazis. My mother's mother, Elisabeth Nathans, was gassed at Sobibor, a death camp on the eastern border of Poland. My father's father, Jules Wynhausen, was deported, and only this year I found out that he also died in Sobibor.

Neither my brother nor I were able to confront the manner of their going. We were aware that our grandparents had died during the war, but we never asked questions about it, as if frightened of straying into a territory that had been sealed off for good. Nevertheless, those unexplained deaths assumed an odd, almost sacred character, as if, in talking about them, we would dissipate the sense of significance that was the mainspring of our identity as Jews.

At school, history was taught in two ways. If it was ancient history, that is, anything that had happened before 1914, it was short on imagery. Ancient history was a stick figure like Commodore Perry sailing to an arrow on the map of Japan. The human element was deleted; the causes and effects were on an epic scale. Modern history, in contrast, had been reduced to hand-to-hand combat, and the combat was mythologized. The history of the second world war was about ennobled Anglo-Saxons like the Rats of Tobruk beating the piss out of the maddened, but cowardly, Turk. Australia's very shores had been under assault, and what with them sneaking right into Port Jackson in midget submarines, the Japanese were easier to bring to mind than the Germans. After all, almost everyone in the class had heard about a soldier who came back from Changi, yellow with malaria and thin as a rail.

Modern history was presented in imaginable snippets, even if it made no sense with its heroes and villains looming up out of nowhere and subsiding just as suddenly. Admittedly, I did not think about it much. It was not my show, though I liked its names. Kokoda Trail . . . Coral Sea . . . They sounded mysterious, alluring. You could visualize someone in a boxtop competition being informed that he had won a ten-day holiday to the Coral Sea, all expenses paid.

Very occasionally in class there was an image of Europe as remote and unreal as a bit of innocent sky and ruined stone painted on a scrim, and then I would wait for Hitler to pop up, slithering to the edge of my seat, tense with self-importance, as if the war were my particular secret. I wanted to tell them about it, but I couldn't get it into perspective. The little that I knew hinged on odd details. The bunch of violets a stranger gave my mother . . . The sound of soldiers marching on a footbridge overhead . . . The clang of barbed wire at the border . . . It was impossible to translate the private meaning of these emblems. Even so, I must have talked about it to the girls in the gang at school, perhaps exaggerating to fill in some of the gaps. Long afterward, someone from the school claimed to remember the stories vividly. 'You told us how your mother escaped in a haycart,' she said. 'It stirred my imagination. I went on to read *Exodus* and all that . . .' Picturesque though the haycart may be, it does not feature in the actual story.

The Netherlands capitulated on May 15 1940, a day after the bombardment of Rotterdam, and five days after the German army marched across the border. The country had long since been infiltrated by German collaborators who helped identify the so-called enemies of the Reich, a task made easier because the Dutch kept such meticulous records. The anti-Jewish measures were introduced piecemeal at first. Jews were ordered to leave public service jobs. They could not teach in schools. They were not permitted to maintain bank accounts. Early in 1941, they were ordered to carry identity cards stamped with a large, red 'J'. In Amsterdam, a city that prided itself on the extent of its assimilation, the unions called a general strike in protest. The strike was bloodily put down.

From that time on, anti-Jewish regulations were posted frequently. Jews were not permitted to sit in parks and public places. They needed a permit to travel. When my mother's brother, Bram, married Ali, the family had to troop into the town hall in Arnhem to apply and pay for permits to travel by train to the wedding in the north. Jewish homes were raided by night and people were taken away to 'work camps'. By the spring of 1942, several of the Nathans cousins had been deported and the family tried, to little avail, to keep the news from my grandfather, who was gravely ill because he could not get medicine for his heart condition.

After his death, a month later, they went into hiding, or spirited themselves out of Arnhem, with little more than the clothes they were wearing. My mother carried a small basket with a skirt, a blouse, a comb, a brush and a mirror. She did not have false papers. Nor did her companions, her brother, Nico, and his friend, Dolf. They slipped over the frontier, spent the night half-asleep in a hayrick, brushed off as best they could — the sort of detail mum would never leave out of a story — and caught a bus to Antwerp.

To pass for local people visiting relatives, they edged from one town to the next, but that did not make them any less conspicuous when they cut across a field at first light; almost as soon as they were over the border, they were picked up by a couple of

German soldiers. My mother, who spoke fluent French, was interviewed that afternoon by the local captain of the gendarmes, and on the spur of the moment confided to him that she had been involved with the Underground, helping French prisoners of war who had escaped. That was reason enough for her to have been handed straight over to the Nazis, but she had guessed right: the policeman said that he would leave the cells unlocked, and told her where to hide with Nico and Dolf, while the search was carried out.

It all went according to plan; they were aboard the train in Lille the following morning, when a stranger wandering along the platform stopped by the window and tossed in a bunch of violets, with the compliments of the captain. 'Violets,' I marvelled, as a child, because violets were her favorite, and my mother smiled a bit complacently, not above revelling in the gallantry of the gesture which capped her story.

In fact, she slipped away from the Germans again, after being cooped up with them for hours. It happened in a small town in occupied France. Nico and Dolf had gone off together and she was hurrying to meet them at a cafe when the air-raid sirens sounded. Forced to take shelter, she found herself in a cellar, surrounded by German soldiers, who smiled encouragingly and tried to talk to her. 'So I just pretended to cry,' my mother told me. 'It was terrible. I had reason enought to cry but it was hard to keep it up for two hours . . .'

In almost any situation, she can find an incident to suggest that things were not as bad as you might have imagined, but nothing lightens the memory of the longest night of her life, the night that they waited on the demarcation line to dodge into unoccupied France. Someone in the Resistance had led them to a place at the river's edge, under a bridge patrolled by soldiers with dogs that barked at every sound. Too frightened even to whisper, they lay dead-still in the reeds, with big water snails crawling over them. 'Think what we've come through,' my mother told herself, and thought instead about Arnhem, where her mother had stayed behind. 'Think about tomorrow . . .' She was feverish, with a severely infected throat, and could not stop shivering. But when the patrol changed at dawn the three of them waded across the river, so keyed up, all of a sudden, that they kept going for another five kilometres before they hung their clothes on the bushes to dry.

An acquaintance in the Resistance in Lyon talked them out of going on to Spain. Though some Jews had escaped that way — on leaky old boats, even trawlers, that set sail for England — the number had been much exaggerated: rumour fed on rumour among people desperate enough to clutch at straws; but hardly anyone had got through in months, and the refugees picked up in Spain were left to rot in prison. 'You wouldn't have a chance,' said the man in Lyon, instead advising my mother and her companions to try to slip into Switzerland.

Up in the mountains of the Haute Savoie, not far from the Swiss frontier, they found themselves pacing around a filthy little hovel, where rats scuttled across the floor. The peasant who had supposedly gone to find a guide to show them where to steal across the border stayed away for three days, on a binge, returning alone at dawn on the third day, to point them, very vaguely, in the right direction. They walked about sixteen hours, going by mountainous backroads, to the high barbed-wire at the border. The men struggled through, and Nico held the strands of wire together for his sister. When he let it go, the snap of the wire echoed like a rifle shot, and in less than a minute the guard from the Swiss frontier post was after them.

Though they had agreed to scatter, if it came to that, meeting up again at a particular place in Berne, gallant Dolf stayed with my mother, only to be arrested as well. From the frontier post, the two of them were driven to the police station at Geneva in a Black Maria. Somehow it still makes my mother laugh. Though the cold-hearted Swiss put countless refugees straight back across the border — in effect handing some of them over to the Nazis — the policeman who interviewed my mother in

Geneva promised to let her brother stay, if she revealed his whereabouts. To his astonishment Nico was not only picked up, in Berne, but sentenced to three weeks in gaol, on the official charge of deserting his sister. 'Well, it could have been worse,' mum would say, shamelessly. The policeman who had interviewed her seemed to have his hopes. Nothing came of it, but meanwhile, she was shown around Geneva in a police car.

Neither Jules nor I used to ask our parents questions about the war. If they had a drink or two, and reminisced, we listened in silence, aware of the fragile mood of the occasion, unwilling to get in over our heads. It was as if we did not want to know too much, sensing the desolation that the stories covered up. We drew back even further than they did, and they talked about their war as if, against the odds, they had often managed to have a high old time.

They met about two months after her arrival in Geneva. The policeman lost out very quickly to the dark-haired, handsome refugee from Holland who refused to leave her side, even after she was interned the following winter. She was interned in the place of her brother, Bram, who had reached Switzerland at last but was still frail because he had been shot during an escape attempt. Officials dismissed that as if it were just another hard-luck story, and Bram was shipped off to a work camp that all the refugees feared. Unable to get him out any other way, despite a slanging match with the Dutch consul, my mother insisted on swapping places with Bram. Either she was fortunate, once again, or one or other official responded to her pluck. Instead of being assigned to the camp, she and my father were sent to Mont Pelerin, the scene of the adventures that they talked about later on.

Mont Pelerin was a village in the alps, not far from Lausanne. Until reaching the place, by a funicular railway, my parents were unaware that they were to live in a beautiful old hotel that had been requisitioned by the regime. The refugees who happened to be there at the time included a contingent of cabaret artists and actors; some circus people whose children climbed up the curtains to keep in shape; and, at the other end of the spectrum, fashionable, worldly individuals from Dutch families so well fixed, before the war, that my mother associated them with the beau monde.

For some weeks she shared a room with a leading lady of Dutch theatre, whose admirers dropped by in the evenings, throwing themselves across my mother's bed as if she were a block of wood, to gaze adoringly at the star. It would have diverted my mother, who was urbane enough to play along. No-one could have levelled such an accusation at my father, who had been in his element in a dorp in the provinces, and washed up in Mont Pelerin to share a room with Billy Duveen, a nephew of the Duveen who had been the most spectacular art dealer of all time.

Thrown together like that, my parents formed alliances with people who were to provide a benchmark of their own experiences. 'Well, of course, you know who we were with in Switzerland,' my mother said now and again, indulging a small vanity, and reminding us that she had the savoir-faire to fit in with people from all walks of life. That is not to say that the people at Mont Pelerin were merely refined, and mum collapsed into giggles if she happened to recall some of the things that had gone on. She once went into a hotel room to borrow something and, seeing three people in bed together, greeted them airily (as she later reported with pride) before scuttling out into the corridor. My father had also covered himself with glory, if nothing else. He galloped down the hotel stairs, buck-naked and full of booze, moments after being put to bed, during an uproarious party that he was evidently determined not to miss.

The breathless way in which such incidents were recalled evoked an atmosphere of hectic gaiety, with everything heightened and faintly unreal, as if the refugees had conspired not to focus on the immediate past or the ominous future.

Nevertheless, my parents had not been in Mont Pelerin for

long when they decided to marry, doubtless for love, though what they will mention in explaining the whole thing is that someone had loaned dad the fifty French francs he needed to pay the mayor in Chardonne, the nearest town of any size, to perform the civil ceremony. Neither of my parents are believers, but they did not think twice about following that up with the religious ritual. The rabbi who officiated was an old man sheltering from the August sun under a broad-brimmed black hat, and for once this traditional sight could not have been more of a comfort. Though he had come all the way from Zurich, he stepped off the funicular with a bottle of kosher wine clutched under each arm, and proceeded to tell my mother about the people in her family he had met, in Amsterdam, before the first world war.

No more than a few weeks after the wedding, my parents and five other couples left with Andrea Waldegg, the Swiss in charge at Mont Pelerin, on an official mission. People from the Theresienstadt concentration camp were being released in exchanges with German prisoners of war, and Waldegg's team went to clean up long-closed hotels in readiness for them, first going to Vico Soprano, a village wedged in a narrow valley between the Swiss and Italian alps.

That alone was enough to frighten some of the people from the camp, who arrived, and were still milling about outside the hotel when one of them, an unexpectedly sprightly old man from Poland, peered up at the alps in fear. 'Are there also lions and tigers up there?' he asked in Yiddish. A couple of days later, the same man came to see my mother, who ran the kitchen, and informing her that he was a tailor, said that the poor wretches who had been in the camp with him needed their clothes stitched and pressed. He wondered if it would be all right to hang a couple of suits to dry in front of the fireplace. When she went to the kitchen, the following morning, my mother stared in amazement for a moment before she burst out laughing. Washing lines criss-crossed the room, and clothes hung everywhere.

Theresienstadt was for an 'elite' among the victims of the Nazis. Conditions were supposed to be less ghastly than at the other concentration camps, and just what this might have meant soon emerged at Vico Soprano, for although there was more than enough to eat, the people from the camp kept sneaking out to the garbage tins to look for potato peelings.

Some sort of order was established in about a fortnight and Waldegg's team moved on, and then moved on again, to St Nicholas, a village near the French frontier that was so isolated and primitive that the locals hid from strangers. That was only one of my mother's grievances when she was left there, alone, to regulate life at the hotel.

'It was dreadful,' she said long afterwards, 'just dreadful. Those people came out of the concentration camp and after a week, no, ten days, they became incredibly difficult and demanding. This one wanted more sun in his room. That one wanted less. They never stopped complaining . . .'

My father had volunteered as soon as he arrived in Switzerland, but was not called up until after the invasion of Normandy. In September 1944, he joined the Princess Irene Brigade, a detachment of strays from the Netherlands by then with the British forces under Montgomery. Early the following year, my mother left Switzerland with a friend whose husband was also in the army. They reached Brussels at about the time of the Battle of the Bulge, and stayed for a while. To her surprise, my mother managed to secure a letter signed by Prince Bernhard, son-in-law of the Dutch queen, instructing military personnel to give her all possible assistance. Nothing could have been more useful: with Allied troops on the move, almost everywhere that she went, my mother could cadge rides, even from stiff-necked British officers reluctant to share their jeeps with civilians. She had fled Holland as a non-person, and returned three years later flourishing a document that opened doors.

First she found my father. The Princess Irene Brigade was in Zeeland, with the troops mopping up. While they were camped, my mother stayed nearby, with the harbourmaster of a small town from which everyone but he and his family had been evacuated, Prince Bernhard's letter was not quite enough for the harbourmaster, who insisted on seeing a wedding licence before my father was permitted to visit. In the evenings he turned up with meat, butter and chocolate from the army stores. He also brought a Colt .45 he had traded with an American soldier, and was showing it to the others one night when it went off unexpectedly and shot a hole in the floor.

The gun was never fired again, as far as I know, though my mother had it with her for protection when she moved into the farmhouse in Heer. Before moving in she hitchhiked to Arnhem. 'It was sinister,' she was to tell me. 'The city was evacuated and almost no-one had been allowed back, although the fighting had stopped. A few thin dogs and cats sniffed around in the rubble. Everywhere you saw half-bombed houses, with broken pieces of furniture, or a piano sticking half-out of a wall . . .' but in the Nieuwstad, strangely enough, she ran into someone from her old street who told her that her mother had left money with another neighbour, in case any of them came back.

My grandmother had insisted on staying in Arnhem to keep in touch with her mother, a stubborn woman then in her eighties, who refused to move, right to the end, when she pushed a German soldier down the back stairs of her apartment building and was promptly shot to death. It happened not long before my grandmother was deported. Neighbours betrayed the people hiding her, in the attic of a house, on the outskirts of Arnhem.

Somehow my mother heard about it while she was in Switzerland. Inevitably, her grief was complicated by guilt. The doctor who treated her ulcers, several years later, told her to try to forget, and perhaps it was only from then on that she spoke of the past as if it were usually just a question of managing.

In the spring of 1945, shortly before the Liberation, she moved into the farmhouse in Heer that my father had described to her in every detail. It had always been his home, but after my grandfather was deported the farm had been taken over by a collaborator, a man called Kusters, who seemed to have had no trouble at all in getting the municipal authorities to sign the place over to him. Getting it reversed was a different matter, and my mother had to badger council officials every day, for weeks on end, before they did what was right.

Though Kusters had been gaoled for collaborating, his wife and some of her pals were still in the house. Nevertheless, my mother moved in upstairs and began a campaign to dislodge them, first pocketing the big key to the front door. The house was flush with the pavement. Unable to go in the door, the people downstairs climbed through a front window. It was quite a sight at night, when American and Canadian soldiers parked their jeeps on the pavement and hopped straight in through the window, with their party favours, liquor and Lucky Strike cigarettes. 'I don't think they came to have English conversation,' my mother said, when I asked what had gone on. She barricaded her bedroom door at night, wandered around the rest of the time as if the other people did not exist, and tipped them out at last.

Discharged from the army three months after the Armistice, my father found it difficult to adjust. He had always been quite a lad, he drank in earnest, and he had some scores to settle. On at least one occasion, he was lucky to stay out of gaol, because he slugged an off-duty policeman, an inspector of police, who approached him in a cafe in a nearby town. The cop, a collaborator, had betrayed my father's brother, Georges, who was shipped off to a concentration camp and died of typhus in the last week of the war. It might have been so much water under the bridge. 'Let me buy you a drink,' the man shouted, insistently. My father punched him, but that was not the end of it, because the cop fell, cracking his head against the bar. The charges against my father were dropped in due course: no-one in the cafe admitted to having seen a thing.

What with one thing and another, I was neither conceived nor brought into the world in an atmosphere of serenity. I was born at home, at dawn, on June 23 1946, but the real commotion occurred down below four or five hours later. Kusters, who had just been released from gaol, was at the door with a policeman to reclaim what prison officials still listed as his address. Our neighbours detested him — he had sold all the milk from the farm to the Germans instead of keeping some back to barter with them — and they stood around shouting at him to get lost.

The woman from next door, who had helped my mother around the house for a few days, positioned herself at the window with the heavy, old-fashioned baby-scale, ready to drop it on his head. My mother slipped the Colt .45 under her pillow in case he managed to get upstairs, but after a bit she could not bear the suspense, and padded over to the window in time to see Kusters slinking off ignominiously, with the policeman just ahead of him and the neighbours close behind.

The Kusters reappeared once more, only to have their suitcase slung out on the street, and then things might have quietened down, but for my father — he was still wild enough, several years after the war, to get into brawls if he happened to have been drinking. Perhaps it was understandable in a man accustomed to expressing his hurt by lashing out, but my mother came to a different conclusion. Fed up with it, she at last gave him an ultimatum: he could stay in Heer, on his own, or start all over again, away from his old haunts; and though it was often dressed up a bit, as a move to further our opportunities, that was how we came to emigrate to Australia.

FIVE

The Lost Tribe of Curl Curl

In the years immediately following our arrival in Australia, we often spent Sunday afternoons in winter at the soccer, watching 'our' team, Sydney-Austral. I would have a tiny orange ribbon in my hair. My brother would have a tiny orange pennant. This was none of our doing, and we spent much of the match trying to make ourselves invisible, while dad went off to talk with compatriots of his from Limburg, who spoke in a thick, incomprehensible dialect.

The Dutch all went to the Sydney-Austral matches. We were sure to be surrounded by people who recognized us, or, more likely, recognized the person seated between us, an older woman we politely called 'tante', although she was not an aunt at all. It was impossible to avoid her — she and her husband usually came along in our car. Her husband, a wee, modest man with a quiet, sly sense of humour, had a concentration camp number tattooed on his forearm. He worked at home as a tailor, making dark suits for all the men we knew, and people seemed to like him well enough to contend with her.

Our 'tante' was a restless mountain of flesh who wore a microscopic cameo on a bosom strangers gaped at in awe. Not only was she a merciless gossip, she never stopped talking, except during the tense bits at the soccer match, when she drew herself in, silent for a split-second, in readiness for the voluminous expansion which followed a Sydney-Austral goal. Despite her size, she was the first up on her feet. The immense orange banner she carried was already unfurled. Holding it up high, she swayed from side to side. 'Hup, Holland,' she bellowed, while my brother and I cringed beside her. 'Hup, Holland . . .'

Complaints about it at home did not get us very far. Switching to Dutch, the language which she used to stake out a moral position, my mother would tell us not to be so unkind, for as we knew, the poor woman was 'nervous'. This was shorthand for having had a hard time in the war. It was not to be questioned and we would be back at the soccer, two or three weeks later, trying to hide as the biggest orange banner that anyone had ever seen waved over our heads.

The Jews we ran into those days were Dutch, and there was no knowing that our universe was a statistical aberration. That is to say, ninety-nine point something per cent of the Dutch flocking to Sydney were not Jews and ninety-nine point something per cent of the Jews were not Dutch, leaving a freakish sample, a handful of people whose allegiances wavered, though they thought of themselves as Dutch, first and foremost.

Instead of establishing a beachhead in Sydney they dispersed, but as a rule, favoured the north side of the city. Several of the families moving briskly up the social scale had gone to live in Cremorne, or neighbouring Clifton Gardens, in big, old-fashioned houses with velvety lawns and ancient trees from from which ferns sprouted in bark-covered baskets.

But my sense of our social standing was hazy, to say the least. I would not have dreamed of comparing our situation to that of any native-born Australian. Class was defined in relation to other Jews, and the Dutch belonged to an elite, or so my parents gave me to understand. The baggage they had brought with them to Sydney included a prejudice they would not have recognized for what it was, and they were probably typical in believing themselves to be a cut above anyone from 'the east'. In our case, all of Russia was mysteriously excluded from this system of classification, very possibly because my mother liked to maintain the curious fiction that one of her ancestors grew up in

Odessa, on the Black Sea, and went west with a troupe of trained bears. Loosely-speaking, that left the Polish Jews to look down on, if for no other reason than that they conversed in Yiddish. I was under the impression that it was a makeshift language spoken by people who did not know how to behave without making other Jews ashamed of them. In the ghetto, they had worn black clothes and mumbled together, needlessly inciting the wrath of the anti-Semites, who would eventually take it out on us, too.

In actual fact, Yiddish — spoken by more than ten million people before the war — was the language which had sustained Jewish culture, and those who spoke it had little but contempt for the so-called Jews from the west, who did not. Knowing as much, nowadays, only manages to complicate my reaction. I have not altogether shaken off the old prejudices, for instance, about the Hasidim, fundamentalists who not only wear black clothes and mumble together, but present Gentiles with an image of Judaism that makes assimilated Jews most uncomfortable, doubtless because we are ambivalent about ourselves.

It did not occur to me for a long time that the sense of unease that I stifled as a child (or circumvented, by misbehaving instead of trying to fit in), was related to what my parents had failed to say about being Jewish. The question was not so much ignored, as shelved. Of course I knew what I was meant to do: I was neither to conceal my Jewishness nor to make a show of it, as if being a Jew was a bit like wearing clean underwear every day; you knew it was there (in case of a traffic accident), but you did not have to tell the world about it.

I found out later that other children were given a series of warnings before they went out amongst Gentiles; even a birthday party was fraught with danger, because a Jewish kid could blacken the name of the whole race by accidentally taking the biggest piece of cake on the plate. Luckily no-one had said anything like that to me. I was an insistently noisy child always trying to claim the centre of attention, and at home I fitted right in. At family parties with the uncles present, they all competed for attention, shouted to be heard and argued for the sake of argument. They debated angrily over trifles, disagreeing at full volume, for instance, about the merits of a particular brand of petrol. Unobservant in our turn, we children failed to notice that other grown-ups shouted in private, not in front of witnesses. Perhaps it's unfortunate for a writer to start out in life around people convinced that taking stock, like standing still, was dangerous, but there it was; conversationally-speaking, they always sped ahead.

Some distant connections of my mother's were said to be prone to suicide, and none of us were at all surprised, later on, when the daughter of the family fetched up in Tibet with a guru. The tendency towards introspection had obviously been inherited, like sickle cell anaemia, and just look at where it led you.

We had no suicides, apart from dad's aunt in Germany, Jenny, who shot herself after Hitler was elected. We did not even have a philosopher in the family, though we congratulated ourselves about mum's brother, Simon, who wore pebble-thick glasses and had played in a bridge tournament with Omar Sharif. Uncle Simon had stayed in Arnhem. It was not until we met up again, years later, that I found out that the family intellectual exhibited a fatal flaw: he was related to us. He shouted like the other uncles, only louder. His conversation was a series of opinions interrupted by other people's opinions. He used facts as we did, brandishing them aloft only to clear a path in the conversation. He had more stamina than the rest of us, however, and when I chided him for interrupting for the umpteenth time, he looked puckish behind his glasses, but said without hesitation that Napoleon could listen to three conversations at once.

It didn't occur to me or my relatives that I was noisy and pushy, *just like a Jew*, because I was just like them — an echt Nathans, for whom all social life was a performance, verging on a compulsion. The Nathanses would have been astonished to hear that their behaviour, on occasion, fitted the stereotype. They thought of themselves as originals and they did not doubt that they could bend the rules, a bit.

My mother had never hesitated to adapt the Christian religion to our requirements. Perhaps that was why we did not give a thought to the implications of celebrating Christmas, until we were sprung with a tree, and all the trimmings. The tree, a pine, was government property that dad chopped down after dark, hesitating every time that we heard a car approaching. At home, done up with cotton-wool puffs and silver twine, it looked just right, like a photograph in the *Australian Women's Weekly*.

I was tidying it up on Christmas Day when the bell rang unexpectedly and a Dutch couple marched in. Behind them was their daughter, Elly, who was in my class at Jewish Sunday school. Although she was eleven, as I was, Elly was faded, even then, and could creep up on you without making a sound. I stayed where I was under the tree, waiting for the earth to swallow me up. Elly, who had not moved either, stood trans-fixed, just inside the loungeroom, staring at the tree as if she had never seen anything like it. 'Oh, I see,' said her father unnecess-arily, adjusting his rimless spectacles. Perhaps he sniffed. The turkey was almost done. 'You celebrate Christmas . . .'

The episode crystallized what I felt about going to Sunday school, and going to Sunday school almost put me off Jews for life. The only synagogue on our side of the harbour was at Lindfield, on the North Shore. The elite — third, even fourth, generation Australians, who took their cues from the anciens riches of the district — did not go out of their way to mingle with the likes of us. In fact, the children whose parents were the congregation's movers and shakers were in one class at the Sun-day school, and those of us from out our way, or from equally unfashionable suburbs like Hornsby, at the end of the northern line, were in another.

Even the playground had its unofficial demarcation line, and we kept away from the little princesses whose court shoes clicked on the cement. Their propriety was astonishing. Their socks did not fall down, their hair ribbons were never limp, and they wore smocked velvet dresses, the like of which one saw only in shop windows. They knew how to behave, of course, and on the morning that I dropped my prayer book, one of them materialized on the spot, to remind me in a penetrating whisper to kiss the book, in penitence.

My brother and I never failed to protest, but every Sunday, for three years, we were transported the twelve miles to Lindfield, to scratch away in a language that seemed as dusty as the Dead Sea Scrolls. The religious rituals rang hollow, even in retrospect. In line with the custom of the time, my mother's grandfather, Simon Nathans, had a Shabbas Goy, who came by on Fridays to light the lamps. The evening he failed to appear, great-grandfather dashed outside to ask the nearest passerby to fill in for him. 'Do you know who I am?' the stranger asked, once he was in the apartment. He was a famous general, or so family legend has it, and as he made to leave, old Nathans bounded down the stairs ahead of him, to light his way by turning up the gas. This was one of our favourite stories — it delighted us to think of the age-old custom dissipated in the excitement of the moment.

We were sometimes encouraged to show our stuff at Friday night dinners. If I said that the occasion was a bit short on religious solemnity, that would not quite convey its nature. The echo of hilarity was unintended, but we could not rush through the ritual without engaging in self-parody. With no kippah in reach, dad would still be fumbling in his pockets for a hanky — to cover his head — by the time that the candles were lit, if we remembered to light candles that night. My mother would make a triumphant entry with the bread that she had left in the kitchen by mistake, a minute too late to catch the prayer for the bread that Jules had just mumbled at breakneck speed. Despite the rumours about cultivated Europeans, we had wine only on special occasions (or with visitors): the Sabbath was not special enough. Instead, in response to the prayer for wine, we wildly waved our empty water glasses and shouted 'Good Shabbas', before the usual benediction from dad, who reminded us how lucky we were to have mum slaving away in the kitchen.

The truth of it is that we cannot stand the tension when we are expected to be serious. It seems to be a rule in my family that all sublime ceremonial occasions will end badly. My bat mitzvah was no exception.

The bat mitzvah is a modern, liberal invention that acknowledges, a little grudgingly, that girls also have a coming-of-age. At Lindfield, it was customary for girls to give a short speech, for instance, on the duties of Jewish women: everyone was aware that a Jewish woman was meant to marry (after a year or two at university), have two children, improve on her mother's recipe for matzo ball soup, and stay out of sight (in the seats towards the back), if she insisted on going to shul; but it didn't hurt to remind people and, according to Rev. W. Katz, the founding rabbi, Lindfield always put on quite a show. 'Guests . . . would remark on the unique experience, the high standard and perfect decorum of the whole congregation at the ceremony, and the family spirit at dinner.'

But the spirit at my bat mitzvah was more like the spirit prevailing at the Defenestration of Prague, which led to the Thirty Years War. Though we shared a table with Elly's family, there had been some procedural dispute beforehand, and that was the last that we ever saw of them. It is unlike my mother to nurse grievances and now, looking back on it, I ask myself if the row with Elly's mum was the last straw — for at Lindfield Synagogue we always felt as if we were poor relations.

I was delighted to leave it behind. For several years I had no formal contact with my own kind (and, at another stage of my life, I was to avoid it, never without the suspicion that I was rejecting them before they could reject me). It did not inhibit me from giving myself airs at school, where I was the official Jew. In that context, I thought of it as a marvel of perpetual, unearned distinction, and I paraded my identity as if I were getting into war paint, just to put the wind up the other tribe.

Miss Knodler, the headmistress of the high school, very often provided the occasion, not least because she was in the habit of using the word 'Christian' as a synonym for all that was right and decent. The school motto, which might have mortified us less if it were in Latin, was 'Truth, Beauty, Light', and in case we managed to misconstrue it, Miss Knodler gave the gloss. 'Our Christian religion is based on TRUTH . . . Christ said, "I am the way, the TRUTH and the LIGHT" . . .'

Yet I doubt that she was devout. In her scheme of things, 'duty' and 'seemliness' were the first two commandments, and Jesus got the nod because the headmistress was an old hand in a system (shaped by ancient sectarian struggles between the Anglicans, the Presbyterians and the Papists) that had awarded the toss to a tepid, 'non-denominational' Christianity. Since it was obvious that the Protestant ethic had prevailed over the supernatural, perhaps only a Jew or an infidel could have complained that the state schools had been left with a state religion, in which worldly excellence (in tunnelball or trigonometry, for instance) was blandly entwined with the generic Christian virtues, as if you could not have one without the other.

Perhaps it would have been less noticeable in the northern hemisphere, but as it was, the academic year ended shortly before Christmas, the Assembly Hall was decked with holly, and Baby Jesus was always there on Speech Night. The swots reluctantly left the stage, with the prizes — copies of books by Kipling or Dickens or Thackeray — hanging like lead weights from their hands, and then it was time for the seasonal festivities, interpreted by Miss Knodler as the excuse for the usual sermon, primped up a bit, of course, to allow for the Spirit of Christmas. Other girls fidgeted in silence against the constraints of time and place and the starchy white frocks that we were forced to wear on Speech Night. I was never silent for long. Provoked, I scoffed in a whisper at every allusion to 'Our Lord'.

No-one was allowed to forget that I was the school's official Jew. I played it to the hilt, though not without asking myself from time to time if I was faking it, a question posed by the existence of the unofficial Jew, a girl called Helen Rootvelt, who was persecuted all along. Supposedly, none of the others knew about Helen, whose family was also Dutch. Her mother, a meek, helplessly apologetic woman who worked at Coles, had nervous breakdowns and people said no wonder, because Mr Rootvelt was a bulky, brutal-seeming man reputed to be cruel to his wife. Hidden in a cellar in Amsterdam during the war, they subsequently could not stand the sight of each other, and Helen was not allowed to forget that she was the reason her mother stayed married.

Though consoled by the idea that her own kind was somehow superior, Mrs Rootvelt warned Helen not to tell Australians that she was Jewish. I was aware of it. When Helen and I were in the same class at primary school, my mother had explained it to me. Jews who profess the faith are sometimes affronted by those who finesse it, but the Dutch are generally more relaxed about the vagaries of assimilation, and what you grew up with as a child whose parents had been trapped in Europe during the war was a loose understanding that denial and complicity shifted from context to context. People who denied their origins, even among their own, were pusillanimous, but the presence of Gentiles changed the picture, and mum said that some people we knew had been so traumatized by the war that they lived in terror of discovery, even in secure Sydney.

I kept Helen's secret, though not without reasons of my own. I was in no hurry to broadcast the fact that we were two of a kind. Somewhere at the back of my mind, I had cast her as my doppelgänger, the spectre that raised all the wrong questions about my identity. She was overweight and almost swarthy, with a faint, darkish fuzz on her upper lip that was evident before any of the other girls reached puberty. They tried not to show distaste, but they did not try very hard, and her place in the gang was even less assured than mine. None too surprisingly, we failed to strike up an alliance, and at the age of ten or eleven I lost some of my innocence because of it: instead of defending Helen in public as I knew I should, I hid behind a careful and unprecedented silence if someone was mean about her.

She made other friends at high school, where she was always in trouble. Of course it was self-destructive, but a teacher faced with a class of forty-five girls did not pause to analyze someone's motives for misbehaving, and Helen confronted people with her unfocused energy and her strength as if expecting them to recoil.

It was as if she never got away with anything — she was accident prone, and the accident that people talked about occurred during our final year. Dozens of girls were on the playing field, practising for the inter-school sports carnival, when it happened. Helen Rootvelt hurled a javelin high in the air. Only the glint of it was visible as it darted down, right on course, and speared Helen Bartle, a lanky blonde high jumper who had wandered across the field unseeingly during an intense discussion of tactics. She looked down at her side for a minute, and keeled over as if she had been pole-axed. It wasn't serious, but her gym bloomers were soaked in mercurochrome by the time that she was rushed off to Manly District Hospital, to have six stitches.

No-one remembered seeing Helen Rootvelt, after she hurled the javelin. Though expected to set a record at the school carnival the following week, she failed to get to the finals.

I met her not long ago. I had looked up some of the people from school, to jolt my memory before I wrote this book. Helen, who had become a history teacher, was considering starting over, as a teacher of the handicapped. She had the easy, equable calm of someone who would not be rattled by a mob of children, and it was obvious that she had mastered her own demons; even so, she said that the prospect of talking about the past had disturbed her sleep. When we spoke about the girls at school, she confused one bland, blonde Presbyterian with another. Perhaps she couldn't tell them apart.

But they brought her to mind with no trouble at all. 'There was that girl, Helen Rubinstein,' said a woman who had been my best friend when we were ten years old. Despite the slip, she mulled over the news that Helen was Jewish, as if pausing to confirm it to herself, before she nodded, slowly. 'I suppose that's right. My mother always said there was something about her.'

SIX
Nice Jewish Boys

Despite the plaintive suggestions that we join a 'Jewish tennis club', neither Jules nor I showed the slightest interest in seeking out our co-religionists, and my mother was startled into action the first time that a boy asked me out. His name was Brian, he was at least an inch and a half taller than I, and we met after the foxtrot in my school's Assembly Hall. Indicating a preference which made me think that there must be something wrong with him, Brian sidled over to ask if he could have the pleasure of 'this, er . . .' After he telephoned the next day, my mother stopped just short of the Torquemada in her efforts to find out about him, but restrained herself from asking if he were Jewish. The question was redundant. He lived in French's Forest, where there are about as many Jews as there are in Mecca.

It took me only three days to get ready to go to the Balgowlah Odeon with him. I thought of it as a historic occasion. Every other fifteen year old in the universe had been putting theory into practice for years, while I sat at home, reading *Seventeen* magazine's advice about how to act on the first date, though all I needed to know, in the event, was how you explained to a boy who had only just managed to inch his arm across your shoulders that your parents insisted on picking you up outside the cinema.

Less than a month later, Jules and I were packed off to summer camp, almost without warning. 'You always liked going to camp,' mum said triumphantly. The camp had some connection with a youth movement called Betar, but further enquiries were fruitless — it was not in my mother's nature to accumulate extraneous information, and she knew everything about Betar that she needed to know. 'What's to ask,' she said, and went on dusting down the suitcases, 'it's a Jewish camp.'

The Betar people were waiting around, out the back of Sydney's Central Railway by Eddy Avenue. Vagrants went there to beg and seedy couples with string-tied suitcases forgot about being hungover and had a row instead. It was one of my favourite places when I was a child. I liked peeking at the Aborigines in gaudy mission frocks, and the widgies with enough teased hair for mice to nest in. The scene had not changed greatly. Men with pinched faces hurried past to buy one-way tickets. The drunks on a visit from nearby Belmore Park lounged about, out of the way of the Betar campers, who were in uniform.

They wore navy-blue shirts with a white lanyard, and a cap — just like the WRAAFs had in the second war — tucked into the shoulder tab. No-one appeared to have warned them against advertising that they were Jewish, because they shrieked '... shalom, shalom ...' if anyone they knew turned up. Jules nudged me, grinning. Several of them were swearing loudly enough for all the world to hear, the first hint that we were to find the campers to our liking. Startling as it was to find out that we had anything in common with other Jews, we very soon felt as if we had known them all along, and within a day or two, my brother and I unselfconsciously declared ourselves to be Betarim. The campsite just outside Sutherland on the southern edge of Sydney was owned by an obscure Christian fellowship: like the Seventh Day Adventists or the Pentacostalists who practised sticking together, we pitched our tents, played volleyball and were prodded along on bushwalks by relentless enthusiasts who had earned their stripes ... but the theory was a bit different, of course. In some quarters, the motivating spirit of Betar was construed as disloyal to our adopted country. We were being toughened up with bush walks and Camp Pie only for the time that we would desert Australia to go to Israel. Betar existed to transform namby-pamby Jewish youth into Zionist warriors, but first, in the words of its dated inspirational material, we had to abandon 'the slovenly habits of the suppressed ghetto Jew'. On the banks of the Woronora River, outside Sutherland, this appeared to mean that one was betraying one's revised heritage by fighting with Ruthie Goldberg about whose turn it was to wash up.

Though there were ballgames and folkdances, much as you might expect, in a decided departure from the routines of the Pentacostalists and Presbyterians, we were taught a supposed self-defence technique. In the process of becoming what the founder of Betar had called 'the new type of Jew', we spent hours flailing away at one another with sticks. No-one ever bothered to explain how stick-fighting, a loosely-adapted martial art, was going to help the new type of Jew in a border dispute with the old type of Arab, but that did not daunt the likes of us. We were the heirs to a militant tradition.

Betar's propaganda traced a direct line of succession from the martyrs of Massada — who had killed themselves instead of being captured by the Romans — to the Irgun Zvai Leumi, one of three underground organizations operating in Palestine at the time of the British Mandate. Betar had been the breeding ground of some of the terrorists in the Irgun, who bombed the King David Hotel in Jerusalem, military headquarters of the British, in one of the bloodier moments of the campaign to dislodge them.

The bombing, in July 1946, reverberated as far away as Australia, where even the Zionists blanched a bit, making muted statements to disassociate themselves from the actions of the Irgun. Anti-Zionists, including Sir Isaac Isaacs, a former Governor-General, turned themselves inside-out to convince non-Jews of their loyalty to the British Crown. Indeed, it might have been said that the position of the (Anglophile) Jewish establishment was being threatened on several fronts. The first reffos from the D.P. camps were already sailing towards Australia, and their arrival was not universally welcomed. Newspaper headlines referred to a 'rush of Jews'; rabid politicians said that Australia should not be a 'dumping ground' for what the official racists called 'the refuse of Europe'; and the *Bulletin*, drawing a long bow, linked all Jews to the terrorists in Palestine.

Betar had started in Sydney that year. The sense of timing alone was enough to hint at its posture, and though the situation had changed by 1961, the message had not. Betar was as belligerent as ever. Ze'ev Jabotinsky, its founder, had said that he was willing to die for his country, and so, in theory, were we. The trouble was that playing soldiers in the Sutherland Shire was a bit short on dramatic interest. In its place, the boys had invented a martial sport, aimed at the enemy within.

Our families called in on Sundays (with fresh supplies of kugel, boiled chicken and chocolate), and someone occasionally turned up in a Volkswagen or a Mercedes. If the boys were in the neighbourhood, across the river from the campsite, they chucked pebbles at the cars. Visitors who brazened it out would get back to find the tyres let down, or the windows chalked with graffiti.

All in all, it may not have been the summer camp our parents envisaged, but they were grappling with more urgent claims: we had reached our teens and it was time to start sifting through the potential partners. My mother will not admit to so banal a motive, but if she secretly hoped to steer me towards some nice Jewish boys, she succeeded all too well.

On my third night in Betar, I was felt up by a nice Jewish boy called Les. I don't know what happened to Les, but it was archetypal experience for me. I was astonished that I was normal enough to provoke this pawing. Years later, I might find myself in bed with one or other bloke who had absolutely nothing to recommend him, except that he had decided that I was desirable. Sheer gratitude was unlikely to inspire a second encounter, but it often explained the first. Of course, I was always aware that relief may be quickly upstaged by regret.

Les got a finger, or was it a thumb? into my Cottontails. Within five minutes I was sure there must be some outward sign of this stain on my character. We were at it again the next night, however, jammed in a foxhole on the perimeter of the campground, grinding away between arguments. Les felt short-changed. With so unexpected a score ('downstairs, inside') on the first night, he imagined that the nights to come would produce significant progress. He was wrong. When he started unzipping himself, I sat up resolutely. The spirit of the times prevailed over the heat of the moment: I saw myself as the reliquary of Les's masculine drives, and him as the subject of great, if edited, stories, to tell the girls at school.

During the day, Les and I hammered away instead at tent pegs. Having discovered that I could pitch a tent as fast as any of the boys, I wanted to maintain my form. I did not notice that the other girls were too shrewd to compete in this league. If we went out hiking, they let themselves be helped up the rocks, or waited until some weedy, pimpled gallant had run back and hurled himself at the lantana, to clear a little path. Occasionally a girl capable of exploiting her appeal would stumble, moaning softly and enticingly. In fact, a precocious twelve year old called Marsha had already taught herself to faint, though we waited in vain for her to topple into the river, or off a cliff.

It was only one of the distractions on excursions that doubled as a chance for us to show off, parading in uniform as if daring some anti-Semite to spring from the shadows. Although it was inconceivable that the average citizen of the district had heard of Betar, let alone taken a stand against it, if we ran into the locals we fell into line, marching so exaggeratedly that it might have looked, to the untrained eye, as if we were practising the goose-step.

Betar's mythology encouraged us to think of ourselves as rebels united in a dangerous cause. The feeling of camaraderie was as new to me as the sense of intimacy that came from being with people whose origins were more-than-half familiar. Ina Klein, my closest friend in Betar, was also Dutch, but lived in the eastern suburbs, around boys that she could bring home without being disinherited. I had the impression that she saw more Jewish boys than the emcee at the Central Synagogue dances. Several afternoons a week, she and other girls from her school put on white lipstick and went to Bondi Junction, where a swarm of Jewish teenagers hung around outside Grace Brothers, smoking furtively, and arranging to meet the following Saturday on the Jerusalem Steps at Bondi Beach. It was a sphere of life of which I knew nothing at all, until I joined Betar.

The organization wasted no time in promoting the raw recruits — fourteen or fifteen year olds who survived a camp, to come back for more, were ordained as 'madrichim' (leaders) — and so, in our first year in Betar, my brother and I spent Sundays in uniform travelling clear across the city to Allawah, a suburb on the Illawarra line we had never heard of until we received our marching orders from the movement.

To further the cause at Allawah we played ball games with the children, forced them to listen to stories about the heroes of the Irgun, and danced the Hora. Then we made our way to Betar headquarters, in a rundown old mansion at Edgecliff, where eighteen year olds subjected us to the same routine.

An atmosphere of anticipation livened up the meetings. Now and again a latecomer burst in excitedly to say that he had been jostled by a couple of creeps who followed him off the bus. The boys who rushed out with him to give chase would come back twenty minutes later, looking crestfallen. It left them conjuring encounters with imagined enemies out of sidelong glances and scraps of conversation. I never heard it suggested that any kid in uniform would have been taunted by other teenagers. It did not occur to us that the natives were more or less unaware of our existence.

In the spring, the film *Exodus* had its premiere in Sydney. Our organizers interpreted it as an opportunity to celebrate Betar's glorious past. In 1938, in reaction to the British mandate's quota system restricting the number of Jews allowed into Palestine, Zionist leaders set up several illegal immigration schemes. Betar shipped out about 7,000 refugees in the first six months of 1939. *Exodus*, the story of one of the refugee ships, could not be ignored — our predecessors had organized transports, shepherded refugees to the ports, and manned the boats — and we also had our part to play. It involved weeks of rehearsal and endless drill.

On the night of the premiere, about fifty of us marched in uniform along Pitt Street, and arranged ourselves as an honour guard on the pavement outside the theatre. The guests stepping from taxis stood and stared. 'They didn't expect anything like this,' Ina Klein whispered between closed teeth, as if she were trying not to move her facial muscles. I said nothing, for once. I was so close to suffocating with pride that it was hard to breathe. 'Navy cadets,' a man going past said to his little boy. 'They have them for the Governor.' He looked again. 'I don't know what the girls are for . . .'

We pretended not to hear the comments, staring straight ahead, expressionless as soldiers, even after a famous disc jockey, a small man with a weathered face, walked past as if inspecting the ranks. So did the cinema manager. 'Who's in charge here?' he called out, before asking if we could stand on the other side of the red velvet rope. Luckily we were too full of ourselves to notice the absurdity of the situation.

The absurdity was inevitable, for in a sense we were enacting a private drama that had no public meaning. Betar gave us a claim on our complicated inheritance. We were Jewish because our parents were, or, to be precise about the counterbalance to assimilation, because Hitler had defined their Jewishness for them: as children of the survivors of the war, we were expected to affirm what our parents had endured by conceding our identity. It was the traditional Jewish equation — if we denied the legacy as they interpreted it, we denied the suffering. What it meant to my generation was more or less what it meant to Israel when its leaders made the same argument about the security of the state: conflict on several fronts. Inevitably engaged in sporadic hostilities with our parents, we meanwhile imagined ourselves to be fighting certain battles on their behalf.

Betar's bloody-minded rhetoric lured some individuals who were anything but joiners, and for them, the organization functioned much as a street gang — it gave them the excuse to go out looking for likely skirmishes. Eddy Adamek joined Betar when he was twelve. Long afterwards, he was to tell me that if he thought about the war in those days, he could not come to terms with the fact that Jews had acquiesced in going to certain death. What it made him feel about being Jewish, as a child, was a sense of shame, a little lessened by any opportunity for retribution. If someone at Bellevue Hill primary school called him a name like 'fucking Jewboy', Eddy chalked up one for our side.

I first met him when he was fifteen, and built like a front-row forward gone to seed. He spoke out of the side of his mouth, and in his quieter moments, kept knocking the knuckles of his right hand into the palm of the left. Betar suited assertive types; even so, Adamek and a few of his friends made the rest of us a little nervous. Anyone familiar with the coordinates of the local community would have deduced that Betar had managed to attract the only three Jewish boys in Sydney who could have qualified as lairs, even if they had been Gentiles.

The first time I saw Adamek's best friend, Fred, I assumed that he belonged to some undocumented sub-species of degenerate Jews, and that was about right. He was a bodgie. When he was with his mates, you imagined them draped over milkbar pinball machines, or shagging shiksas. His mum and dad sold tv sets at Bondi Junction, but Fred looked like a greaseball who had come from the underprivileged suburbs by way of Sicily. His curly, black hair was slicked into a duck's tail. He was on the plump side, but he went to the Temple Emanuel dances in a green checked suit with pegged trousers and, on the rare occasions that he dropped into Betar meetings, wore gold chains showing under the blue shirt. If he caught you peeking, he stared back with an expression of fixed contempt that made Brando's scowl seem sissified.

People sometimes wondered aloud why he came at all. Doubtless it was because he identified with Betar's bias. The mentors of the movement in Israel were men to whom violence had been the only means to an end, and if ever push came to shove in peaceful Sydney, our hoods were ready to reason with their fists, their boots and the tyre-iron from the family Holden Fred had souped up before he was old enough to get a driving licence.

He had drifted away from Betar by 1964, when Adamek, among others, started putting theory into practice. Big Ed still dropped into the meetings in Edgecliff, once in a while, but his henchmen had departed the scene and he found it lacklustre. A newspaper article about the local Nazis led him to conceive of another divertissement, and with nothing better to do on a Sunday night he and his cousin George dropped in, prudently parking the car about a mile from the Nazi headquarters, an old house in the working-class suburb of Ashfield.

The Nazis' cat was called Cyclon B. That made the boys a bit nervous, and although there was something less than an intimidating detachment of stormtroopers present, one of their four new acquaintances was The Skull, a tall, gristly character with a shaved head who had already made a name for himself in Sydney. He was the loose cannon of the ratbag right, but his pathological liking for violence was kept in check by his inability to concentrate on any one enemy at a time. The Skull, in short, was none too bright.

By the local standards, however, he was officer material, and had been put in charge of security. Neither he nor the Nazi high command, Fuhrer Arthur Smith and Vice-Fuhrer Brian Rogan, expressed the slightest reservation about the latest converts to their lonely cause. Adamek introduced himself as Edward Meller, saying that he and his cousin wanted to start a Nazi party at university. No-one could mistake them for WASPs, but by chance, neither of the Adameks resemble the hebe of National Socialist literature, a febrile, scrawny, hunch-backed creature in black with a beak like Cyrano de Bergerac; after a short, welcoming speech, Arthur Smith awarded them with swastika badges.

They went back week after week, and once appeared in public with the Nazis: a storm trooper had his appendix out and his associates marched in to see him. It was, Adamek said later, 'bloody embarrassing wearing our swastika badges to Ashfield bloody hospital, very bloody embarrassing'. By that stage, he and cousin George were undercover operatives. They had mentioned their exploits to a pal, a Betar loyalist keeping the faith in the police force, who debriefed them and reported to the Special Branch.

The arrangement was abruptly terminated after the Nazis demoted the Skull, replacing him with an exceptional individual who was not only revolted by Jews, but seemed to be able to recognize them. Turning to Ed, the first time that they met, he asked, '. . . and where was that you said your dad was born, son?'

The Mellers did not go back to the house in Ashfield. Three weeks after they had dematerialized, the Special Branch nabbed the Nazi high command, which had kept itself in jackboots by burgling houses in the eastern suburbs. Tempting as it is to credit the detective work of our undercover operatives, there may have been a bit more to it. The Nazis, who had made the mistake of drawing attention to themselves, were also at the centre of a row which blew up at Sydney University after *Honi Soit*, the student paper, ran articles by the fuhrer.

Though I tried not to dwell on the implications I could not

avoid the fuss, because I was a student at the university by then. I had dropped out of Betar, airily dismissing its propaganda, but still drifted around with the old crowd if other social prospects evaporated.

A number of the people who were, or had been, in Betar, met for lunch in the Buttery, an annex of the university cafeteria, occasionally staying on to play poker. Nothing could distract them from a game of poker, but still, the game appeared to have been interrupted when I strolled into the Buttery late one afternoon. Cards lay scattered across the table, and four or five of my friends were huddled over a copy of *Honi Soit*.

Bronstein glanced up. He was the usual ghastly colour, but his protuberant eyes were out on stalks. 'Have you seen your favourite paper?' he said. He and I had argued over the previous issue. 'Fucking rag. Now it's full of articles by the Nazis . . .'

'Listen to this.' It was the voice of authority. Leo, who was built along the lines of an apprentice jockey, had always been in charge of our group in Betar; even the hoods, like Fred, had concealed a grudging respect for him. He was a cardsharp and a genius. A prodigious poker player, he might stay up all night gambling, and still sweep the field in a history exam a couple of hours later. 'I don't believe it,' he muttered. 'Smith, the fuhrer, says that the answer to the Jewish problem is deportation. "A so-called final solution, i.e., by genocide, is not at all acceptable." Not at all acceptable,' he said again, grinning mirthlessly so that you saw nothing but the bones of his face.

'Deportation?' I tried to picture it. All of us banished to Norfolk Island. The clique from the Cosmopolitan in Double Bay sloughing their mink stoles under the shedding pines. 'Come on, Leo. You can't take it seriously.'

But I felt queasy all the same, and not about the star of the Ashfield SS. In fact, trying to conjure up an image of Fuhrer Smith was light relief. The white trash of any Aryan nation, with pitted skin and the tussocky hair that people want to tug at, expecting it to come away in their hands. Out of uniform he was sure to wear a mustard-coloured suit with brown stitching on the lapels, and to look humble at just the wrong moment. He couldn't even revise history without being tepid about it. '. . . i.e., by genocide . . .' What a way to put it.

'Shouldn't it be "e.g., by genocide"?' I was staving off something else, a feeling of being exposed. The situation forced one to take sides, and I had a few reservations about my side. I read over Leo's shoulder. 'I mean it's not exactly *Mein Kampf* is it . . .'

'Jesus,' said Bronstein disgustedly, and they talked instead about the protest meetings being organized. Action against the newspaper was already in the wind. An article in a previous issue had alleged that the Jews themselves were to blame for anti-Semitism, because they favoured each other in financial deals and monopolized the rag trade. Doubtless it revealed the exaggerated sensitivity of the Jews that they were starting to think of *Honi Soit* as a primer to *The Protocols of Zion*. They were not alone, however, in refusing to dismiss articles promoting the Nazi cause as a stupid prank. McDermott, the student editor, met his critics and a volley of rotten tomatoes at a demo in a university lecture theatre, but more distant forces were at work, and the Students' Representative Council suspended him as editor a fortnight later. It was no more than he deserved for being disingenuous. He had claimed the freedom to bait the Jews and cried foul when they retaliated just as he might have guessed they would.

Nor, to my way of thinking, was there much to be said for his official opponents. The sentinels on our side were square, self-righteous and humourless. Their style was enough to condemn them. I could not forgive them for presuming to speak for me. I did not want to be associated with the earnest conformists of the university's Jewish Students' Union, who took their cues from the Jewish Board of Deputies. Of course the old guard had inevitably over-reacted. Indeed, instead of ignoring a flagrant attempt to provoke them, they whipped themselves into a frenzy about 'the recent emergence of anti-Semitism from many quarters' (not just the university precinct and the fuhrer-bunker at Ashfield, mind you, but the Town Hall parking lot, where someone had daubed swastikas on car windows during the Israeli independence day celebrations).

'Well, they slipped through your defences,' I told my brother, as soon as I heard about the business in the car park. Not only was Jules still in Betar, he was one of a gang of vigilantes. It was a secret organization. People were not supposed to notice a bunch of teenagers fooling around with walkie-talkies at the back of any crowd of Jews. During the independence day formal they skulked around the Town Hall, dressed in black skivvies and black jeans. Doubtless intimidated, the bomb-throwers stayed away in droves and even the graffitist had not got clean away. 'We know who it was,' Jules mumbled darkly and, refusing to say more, he went into the garage to do some push-ups.

He and his pals officially belonged to something called The Hakoah Wrestling Club. That, at least, was what it said on the back of the tracksuits donated by a retailer in the rag trade. The whole thing had been organized by a paranoid with para-military leanings, who rounded up volunteers from the Zionist youth movements and started knocking them into shape. The routines were rigorous and, as a respite from the ten-mile runs and the twenty-mile marches, they were taught an elementary ju-jitsu backed up by street-fighting tactics.

Many year later, I asked Jules if they had really gone around beating people up. 'Nah, c'mon,' he gave me a look that said it was a silly question. 'I mean there wasn't anyone to beat up. Nothing ever happened.'

Still, he had stuck it out for a while revealing, if nothing else, that he had more staying power than Ed Adamek, who threw in the towel after a training session or two. The first time he showed up in Centennial Park for the training, the instructor lined them up facing each other and told them to imagine that they were in a fight. They were to slap each other hard in the face, trying not to flinch. Big Ed hung his head; across from him was a friend of his father's, a man he had known for years. 'Hit me,' the guy said, steadying himself before he lifted his chin. 'I can't,' whispered the Brawler from Bellevue Hill.

They were all to meet one more time. Towards the summer in 1967, the National Socialists spread the word about a large rally in the hallowed Domain in Sydney, on a Sunday, and managed to lure almost every Nazi in the country as well as some promising recruits.

Three cow-cockies in broad brimmed hats who had come on a bus tour from Cunnamulla heard about the rally when they bumped into an old mate from the League of Rights. A few Catholic ladies who could have been confused about the nature of the event wandered around, politely handing out DLP pamphlets. They, in turn, were briefed by a whiskery pensioner with fond, unreliable memories of the old Australian Natives Association, who nonetheless told everyone in hearing about the medal he had been given by the Turks who came to his RSL club.

Even allowing for the unexpected breadth of his support, Arthur Smith must have been startled by the size of the audience. Instead of a few dozen stormtroopers and hangers-on, a tally that would have been sufficient to count the afternoon a success, the fuhrer saw hundreds of young men who were milling about impatiently, eager for the show to start. But without futher ado, he introduced the warm-up speaker, a Nazi on sabbatical from South Africa, who went on and on about the white man's burden, in spite of the heckling from a pair of young Spartacists and the strange restlessness of the crowd. At long last he clambered from the platform into the small area roped off in front of it, and Smith stepped up to the microphone. The fuhrer had shouted 'seig heil' just once when there was a concerted rush towards him.

The rally had been well-publicized. Our lads, who had got

wind of it about a fortnight beforehand, had done some careful planning of their own. Big Ed was with the contingent from the Hakoah Wrestling Club which had inveigled itself into the roped-off area, with the guests and the leading Nazis. The platform was demolished in less than a minute, and then they really waded in. The reinforcements were right behind them. Close to five hundred young Jews had made it to the rally. In fact, most of them had not yet booted into the middle of the melee when the police moved in, perhaps belatedly, as far as Smith's stormtroopers were concerned.

Once the dust had settled, the score appeared to be four-six, our way. Four of the Nazis were carted off to hospital and six of the Jews were carted off to gaol. But it was the court hearing which was the coup de grace. Big Ed emerged from it unable to stop boasting about his sentence. He had been barred from the Domain for three years.

SEVEN

The Alexandria Trio

I had gone to university determined to shake free of the vestiges of my old life and, in the first place, decided to give an impression of great nonchalance. That is to say, I hung the clothes which looked at all respectable in the back of the wardrobe and slouched around from day to day in black stretch pants, a baggy sweater with holes in the elbows and thick, smudged eyeliner. My mother said, '. . . your eyes look like pissholes in the snow,' and I accused her of being conventional, the deadliest charge that I could muster. That may have been our final exchange on the matter for several months, because she and dad were going abroad.

Jules and I were dumped on the family, throwing Uncle Bram's well-run establishment into an uproar. Exaggerating slightly, he claimed that we were treating his place like a cheap hotel, though it was only compared to our compliant cousin that we came and went almost as we liked. The motor of my brother's Vespa whined in the stillness of the night, doors banged at unexpected hours, fights broke out below stairs, where we slept, and on the rare occasions he stayed home, Jules secluded himself in the garage to tinker with his dream machine. 'They picked a fine time to go overseas,' my uncle grumbled occasionally when we were supposed to be out of earshot.

Gaudy photos came from Edinburgh and Amsterdam, with postcard blue skies in places famous for drizzle. On the telephone from Denmark, my mother said that all the women in the

Tivoli Gardens smoked cigars, and that was the least of her revelations. The cafes all had Royal Copenhagen ashtrays and no-one pinched them, she added, before making an unflattering comparison between the average Australian and the honest Danes. It was a sore point. Very soon after she had opened her dress shop, Paris Frocks, people had stolen the ashtrays in the fitting rooms. She was still sounding nostalgic about life in Europe when her voice faded away. Doubtless dad stood inches away from her, telling her to hang up. The only thing that he ever asked on an international phone call was what time it was, over there. 'Damn,' she shouted at him in Dutch, so loudly that I snapped the telephone away from my ear, '. . . . . at uni . . . .'

Perhaps the lines went under water. Gurgling drowned her out. '. . . . . ice . . . . ice ends.'

'What?'

'I said . . . . friends?'

'Well, they're not Jewish, if that's what you mean . . .'

Silence. She would be rummaging around for more coins, but it was too late. We had been abruptly cut off, as usual; the receiver hung from my hand like a dead bird. '. . . and don't keep asking if they're nice,' I said softly, missing her, 'because they're not.'

The few other girls from my school who had gone to university clung together for protection, but I was inclined to avoid them. I wanted to venture into the unknown. I thought that you could start out again, with people who had not made up their minds about you, and as a result I turned into a failed social climber, as an innocent going on eighteen. I had made friends with a girl called Pippa who sank down next to me in an anthropology tutorial, and looked squeamish at the very thought of those old bones theoretically put together as Piltdown Man.

Over coffee, after the class, she came alive, gossiping animatedly about people whose pictures were in the society pages, for all I knew. I had never met anyone like her. She managed to act dazed, almost helpless, so that one found oneself shepherding her to lecture halls with which she must have been familiar, but without a doubt she knew her way around the Foyer, the cafe where campus identities held court. Her brother, who had considerable social cachet, lolled about in the Foyer smiling with benign lack of interest at anyone who spoke to him, but he managed to overcome his lethargy long enough to organize a table at the Arts Ball, a ceremonial rite that his set took for granted.

I went along with high hopes of my escort, a big, broad-shouldered, clean-cut boy from the country, who spoke with great deliberation. He was known in a rather fast crowd for his restraint and I fantasized about shaking him up a bit. Too naive to know that the unassertiveness of the upper classes could conceal certainties long to elude me, I didn't think to allow for good manners.

Much of the wind went out of my sails as soon as we reached the Trocadero. Though the décolletage of my short, dark green dress had been a sensation at a Betar party, the previous summer, the French tart effect was startlingly out of place at the ball. The debutantes were got up in slinky white concoctions which must have cost a packet. No wonder Jim had looked so surprised when he came to collect me. Neither of us said much, but we drank in earnest, and almost all that I remember of the last hour or two of the evening are brief flashbacks, starting at the moment that I slithered off my chair, to crawl around under the table.

Someone had hoisted me back into my chair. 'Everything happens at balls,' said Pippa's brother, before he swam out of sight. A grizzled attendant in grey was fussing around my legs with bandaids. 'Broken glass,' I mumbled perceptively. The cuts were superficial but there was blood everywhere. It seeped through the bandage on my knee. It trickled under the bandaids criss-crossing my shins. It was smeared over his hands. '. . .'s alright,' I said, embarrassed, 'doesn't hurt . . .'. It didn't, either. 'Have a drink.'

Gentleman Jim had disappeared. I knew he was not under the table because I was looking for him when I slid off the chair. I may have dozed off for a bit, because the next thing I can recall is that a man on stage had launched into a speech about Miss Arts. The dance floor was empty. People were back in their seats. Jim was nowhere to be seen. '. . . she has that rare quality — perhaps you would call it charm . . .' said the man at the microphone; he was still blathering on when I leaped up and propelled myself, backwards, into the centre of the empty floor. 'I want to be Miss Arts,' I yowled, 'I want to be Miss Arts . . .'

Understandably reluctant to show my face around the Foyer again, I rejoined the poker players in the Buttery, quickly attaching myself to the maverick in their midst. Moses had been in Betar, before my time, but it was impossible to imagine him doing anything as normal as stick-fighting on the banks of the Woronora. His interests were depraved, enough to fit him out in my mind as an ideal companion. An Indian, whose face looked sallow against the thick, black brush of his moustache, he spoke about Nietzsche in a sing-song voice, and ignored his lectures at university to pursue private research into the occult. Around three, every afternoon, he emerged from his burrow in the stacks of the Fisher Library. In the Buttery, he could hold forth for an hour, barely pausing as he plucked out an extravagantly-annotated work by Nietzsche or Dostoyevsky, to fling it open on the table and read a couple of sentences underlined so often the print had blurred. Inspired, if only to dogged imitation, I had thumbed *Thus Spake Zarathustra* from cover to cover, underlining furiously in spite of my failure to penetrate its fog of Germanic gloom.

Almost everything that Moses said also went over my head. Though his answers were never much use, I insisted on consulting him on practical questions. 'I have to get out of my English tutorial,' I told him one afternoon as the Buttery was emptying out. With the two of us left at the table, we could have what I thought of as ordinary conversation, if only Moses stopped quoting, for a minute. 'Who will rid me of this turbulent priest,' he said.

My tutor, a priest with a cracked, caressing voice, was even fervent about Wordsworth. Tremulous, holier-than-thou Wordsworth turned into a dirty old man before our eyes, '. . . Be this naked stone/ My seat . . .' whispered with no more than the cleric's usual suggestiveness was enough to make the modest girls he badgered with questions blush, but those of us bold enought to judge him a fool had gone to ask for a change of tutor. No dice. The professor's secretary said that he was out. Professor Wilkes was always out, waging war against the Leavisites, and the most that a first-year student saw of him was a glimpse of his long legs striding down the corridor, his academic gown flapping out behind.

'That's what you said last time about the damn priest . . .' I had entrusted my education to a man who had taken an interest in it once, advising me to read *Alice in Wonderland* instead of going to a lecture on statistics. He wasn't convinced that women belonged in a university, probably because he didn't know what to make of them, and he dressed up his skittishness in flights of fancy about the other half of the species, as if it were easier to dream up a universe populated by sirens and harpies than to admit he was frightened of kissing a girl. Never satisfied with half-measures, he had made up his own set of medieval superstitions, breathing life into them with stories about the black arts women liked to practise on men.

I wouldn't have minded having some black arts at my disposal. 'Sometimes when I'm talking and no-one's listening, I feel I've vanished, you know, as if I don't really exist. That ever happened to you?' I was aware that it would get his attention, but still, he glanced at his book with regret. 'Can't we just talk for a minute?' I've been meaning to ask you something all afternoon.' It was unlike me to hold my fire, but I had an odd request to make of him. 'I told you I met that boy yesterday, Stephan . . .'

It had started in a tutorial. I caught his eye, and he preened like a peacock, running a hand through his dark, lank hair. He was olive-skinned, almost swarthy, with a fine, heavy head, and he stared at me from under half-closed eyes, as if opening them would be altogether too much trouble. Neither of us paid much attention to the tutor, an appealing bushy Welshman called Jones, who was showing the class how to strike a fire with stone-age axes, but I was never to get it out of my mind that Stephan looked like a Neanderthal. Nevertheless, his idea of flirtatious behaviour matched mine, and the first thing we did was argue. I could not shake off a sense of being mesmerized.

'I was going to bring him over today, but his mother's had to go to hospital. I guess he'll be here tomorrow, in the afternoon. Thing is, he thinks he's a fucking genius. If he came over, maybe you could, you know, show him up a bit . . .' It seemed only natural to make Moses my proxy in a battle of wits, and I failed to see why he was slow to enter into the spirit of the thing. 'It'll be a cinch,' I said, 'talk to him about the Cabbala, or something.'

It was a brilliant, if unexpected, match and (given their attitudinizing), a sort of shadow play they conspired to maintain long after I was out of a picture. Stephan's flagging hopes of being enlightened at university revived and he, in his turn, was the advance man. Swaggering in ahead at a party he stood waiting as if he expected a burst of applause, and even if it was all front, he generally managed to act as if nothing could bruise his barbaric confidence.

Before we met he had been on the fringes of another crowd of arts students, and having joined forces, we came to spend a great deal of time with them. If I try to single them out in my mind these days, I sift through a series of theatrical poses before any individual assumes an individual shape. In general, they disdained the proprieties, if not the privileges, of their North Shore families and in casting around for a different image, camped it up with affectations that seemed to have been lifted from some Firbankian parody of life at Oxford. Never again would I see so many limp wrists dripping from tweedy jackets. Never again would anyone see so many boys puffing away, girlishly, on Black Russian cigarettes. Not only was it the last gasp of a style long affiliated with artistic pretensions, it was quickly to be replaced by its antithesis. Though the Sydney University Dramatic Society was still a centre of power on campus that year, influence was shortly to devolve to the political radicals: by the late 'sixties, butch boys and girls in blue jeans set the prevailing style, people smoked Drum instead of fussing with Sobranie cigarettes, and only the most nerveless aesthete could have thought of posing as an upper-class twit.

But that year, as I say, almost anyone who wanted to be a decadent intellectual lounged around the Foyer in a cloud of perfumed smoke, before drifting over to the Forest Lodge Hotel, an establishment patronized by both the hearties — engineering students in shorts and long socks, arranged in a solid wall around the bar — and the arties, who stayed in the beer garden until closing time, when the average decadent intellectual was drunk enough to recite lachrymose verse as a hint of the talent that was being bottled up, until he left home, to live in a garret in Glebe. No-one in my crowd had done so, as yet, but we were full of admiration for the students who had moved into dingy flats, not far from the university, and done them up really well with Batik curtains, Batik tablecloths, Batik bedcovers and candles stuck in Chianti bottles. Not only that, they were always giving parties.

'It's a dead loss,' said my friend David, gloomily surveying the wreckage of a party held on a Friday night in the middle of second term. '. . . I asked him to dance and he said people like me ought to be locked up. He used to go to Cranbrook . . .' We were perched on the dining-room table, trying to take no notice of the couple writhing around underneath it. A girl who had removed some of her clothes and wrapped herself in the tablecloth was picking cigarette butts out of the sodden carpet.

I wondered how to distract him. He had dissolved into tears at the end of the party the previous week. '. . . and when he said that I just stood there with my mouth open.'

'It's so depressing when they put the lights on.' I felt flat. Much as I looked forward to appearing at a party, flanked by Stephan and Moses, before long they were among the illuminati cloistered in the shadows, gossiping about some writer no-one else had heard of.

David nudged me. The fellow he had approached was back in the room. Slithering off the table, we danced, whispering together. 'His eyes are a bit squinty, but he reminds me of Selim . . .'

Selim was a minor character in *The Alexandria Quartet*, which we had hailed as deathless literature and turned into a cult, finding likenesses everywhere. Its Alexandria was an improbably exotic locale in which the sun never set on the empire of the senses; like us, its characters talked long into the night about the agonizing complications of love, reeling off poetry from time to time to give some hint of the unplumbed depths of emotions which could not be reduced to anything as banal, say, as tears and kisses.

'All it ever says about Selim is he's impassive. You keep imagining this handsome Arab with a tea towel around his head when he's probably just a short, fat Egyptian . . . 'scuse me.' I had tripped over the girl in the Batik cloth, who was now crawling around on all fours, apologizing at the top of her voice. 'You're a great dancer, toots, but I have to find Stephan . . .'

All appearances to the contrary, we were still at the romantic stage. If he drove me to my uncle's house, close to the cliffs at Dobroyd Point, we sprawled in the Holden under cover of darkness, pressed together so passionately that neither of us noticed the car slowly sliding forward one night; by the time that we came up for air, it was stuck in a little gully and had to be towed out. If we were forced to uncouple ourselves in the bus shelter on Parramatta Road, the lovemaking was continued once I was cradled over the telephone in my uncle's study, whispering languorously, my stomach constricting with desire. Our silences were drawn-out, our breathing became more urgent, and then, without warning, Uncle Bram would be bellowing in Dutch into the telephone upstairs, '. . . for the last time, get off the damned phone'.

'The family wants to know about the greaseball you go out with,' my brother told me, on a Saturday afternoon that we were confined to base. Upstairs, in front of the relatives, Jules had grunted as if he were brain-damaged in answer to any question, before retiring to the garage where he lay back over an oil smudge, staring into space.

The last time he had shown any real excitement was after Cousin Ron begged for a ride on the Vespa, and damn near cata-pulted over the cliff top. There was no love lost between them; instead of sharing Ron's large bedroom, Mister Cool had elected to sleep on a stretcher in the laundry, his feet wedged up against the Whirlpool. At the best of times, he was inclined to react to any attempt to converse with him as if it were an unpro-voked assault, and he was quite capable of retreating into silence for days on end. Our other aunt, who saw no teenagers at close range, was convinced that he needed a psychiatrist. 'All he needs is a kick in the backside,' I'd heard Uncle Bram say when I lurked on the stairs to eavesdrop on a family conference, 'her, too, and if they were mine, I'd sort them out in a minute . . .'

'Well,' said Aunty Nan, 'we saw it coming.'

The family had never hesitated to tell my mother that she had been too lax with us. Upset at first, she eventually came to think of it as amusing. 'I'd be embarrassed to tell the aunts,' she said, if we gave her cheek. But she had also laughed off the idea of our looking after ourselves while she was abroad.

Both of us had rebelled. Jules, who was the more liable to

store up resentments, did so secretly by playing truant. Perhaps because he was a school prefect, he had managed to work out a system for covering his tracks, and he checked in for roll-call, first thing in the morning, before going on his way. He hung around the Betar office in Edgecliff for the remainder of the day or took to the hills, riding his motor scooter up the Pacific Highway to a place in the bush, where he sat watching the construction crews who were blasting the rock in the path of the new expressway to Newcastle. Not even I knew that he was wagging school four or five days a week. He kept things to himself, though he must have known I wouldn't tell on him — from the time that we were old enough to talk, the punishment for misbehaving had generally been less severe than the punishment for ratting on each other.

Interrogated about my private life he would have clammed up, but in my opinion, it never hurt to ask. 'What did you say about Stephan,' I demanded. Moving with maddening slowness, he propped himself up on one elbow and leered at me. 'I said they could probably find out for themselves, catch him with his pants down, next time he parks across the street . . .'

Despite pressure from the rest of the family, Aunty Ali did not make enquiries for about a fortnight. She was more self-contained than the others; it was not in her nature to probe, but at last she forced herself to ask, a shade ironically, about the boyfriend.

'Did I tell you his father's a doctor? They came from Hungary . . .' Everyone knew that Hungarians were beyond the pale. My mother, who considered herself to be free of all prejudice, called them 'horse thieves', and while this posed no immediate threat, there was a staginess to Stephan's charm '. . . and they're not Jewish.'

'Oh, well,' she said offhandedly, 'you know that's not my way of judging people, and of course he's nice.'

I agreed uneasily. The one certainty was that my uncle would detest him on sight. 'Is there anything you want to talk about,

Bet?' Ali was making a valiant effort. She smiled with relief when I changed the subject, but I was left wondering just what she had managed to guess. Not knowing much about sex, I was worried that it would show.

It had all happened a few days earlier. 'Is that all?' I asked, not meaning to sound aggrieved, and he demanded to know what I was talking about. 'I don't know. I thought I'd feel different.' The throbbing inside had almost stopped and the other discomfort was obscure, hard to place. He went away to wash off the blood and I lay there wondering what to do about the sheet. It looked like we had cut up something alive, right there in Jane's bedroom, with the Beatles blaring 'A Hard Day's Night' on the other side of the wall.

A bad sport could have backed out, but I was not a bad sport. On the contrary, when I forgot about being the Jeanne Moreau character in the film 'Jules et Jim', I flattered myself that I was one of the boys. I sympathized with Stephan's raggedy bravado. I could even forgive his lack of foresight. We had only just undressed when he dashed out of the bedroom, holding a skimpy towel around him and shouting that he had to find a condom. It must have taken him twenty minutes to get it on, but then, somehow without warning he was on top of me, banging away as impatiently as a person on the wrong side of a locked door.

'Is that how you're meant to do it?' I gasped, not having the slightest idea. That was his department. Not only had he told me about the other times, he was inclined to suggest that he had been initiated into techniques of lovemaking too rarefied to practise on a mere girl. Under questioning, he had dropped tantalizing hints of his research in the Fisher stacks, where he and Moses read oriental erotica, and rhapsodized about archaic ways of prolonging sex.

'Ow. Stop it, Stephan. That hurts.' No-one had said anything about it hurting. I should have asked Jane, who hung around the Royal George, and told people about having it off with someone in the Bogle-Chandler case. 'Can't you stop for a minute?' I tried to wriggle away. He mumbled something I did not catch, because I was mumbling at him to stop.

The party was still going strong. People did not seem to notice when I sidled into the other room. 'Hey, Jane . . .' She glistened with sweat, looking oiled. Her body kept undulating, though the record was being changed. Fuck it, he could tell her about her sheet. 'You seen Stephan?'

Her hoarse laughter was prolonged, unnatural. My friends had mythologized Jane, doing such a thorough job of it that a desperate eighteen year old had re-emerged as a romantic figure. Being subject to fits of despair only added to her reputation, and she was said to resemble Justine, the intense, larger-than-life heroine of *The Alexandria Quartet*. Though that was going too far, I was sure that she could have told me a thing or two about love. I could not shake off a sense that I had failed to grasp the essentials. Self-doubt was crystallizing into a conviction that there were mysteries that refused to reveal themselves to me. I wondered if she were mocking me. 'What's so funny? I just asked if you'd seen Stephan.'

'I thought he was with you.' She danced away, still laughing. 'They're in the garden,' someone said, 'him and Moses, talking about bloody black magic.' In the car, driving home, he studied his left profile in the rear vision mirror, and kept his hands to himself. Neither of us had much to say, but I couldn't stop myself from asking what he and Moses were doing out in the garden. I had caught a glimpse of them, prancing around the lantana at the back fence.

'We made grass nooses for our pricks,' he said, so smugly that I fell silent until I was about to get out of the car. 'David and I are going to live in an old hotel in Tangiers,' I said, comforting myself with the thought that I would never let a man touch me again.

The mood passed, and several days later I asked a doctor for the Pill, then famous as 'the free love formula'. Determined in advance to brazen it out, I went to consult the family doctor who was at Dee Why, a washed-out looking suburb stretched between the sand dunes and the spires of too many churches. The churches were all modern. If there was a God, I thought irritably as I got off the bus, he should have been offended by the competitive gleam of all those aluminium spires.

The family doctor was away. His partner, Dr S., had thin, colourless hair combed over the bald patch, and a thin smile. His paternal over-familiarity might have warned me, but I was too nervous. 'I know your daughter,' I said, and immediately wished I hadn't. He would not approve of someone from Manly Girls' asking for the Pill.

'But why do you want this oral contraceptive, Miss Winhoser?' His excuse of a smile was menacing. I should have remembered that he was a Roman Catholic. Though it looked as if he were about to enquire into the details of my sex life, he contented himself with giving a speech. Because I was only eighteen, he said, he would not consider prescribing a contraceptive unless he had talked it over with my parents. He chewed on every word with pleasure, and I was naive enough to believe he was quoting the law. Indeed, I was to wait until the day of my twenty-first birthday to ask another doctor for the Pill. Doubtless it was superstitious, but so was crossing your fingers when you hoped you weren't pregnant.

The question of contraception was not all that was left up to chance, and Stephan and I spent about half our time together looking for somewhere to make love. If we failed to argue tempestuously afterwards, it was because the exigencies of teenage lust found us in dismal surroundings, sprawled on the bare boards of the half-built house across the street from my uncle's house, or kneeling on the cold, damp earth behind some bushes at a party. Once, right after a tutorial, we locked ourselves into a tiny, pitch-black gardener's shed under the stairs leading to the Nicholson Museum. Too frightened of spiders to lean against the wall, I lost my balance and came within inches of being impaled on a rake. In exploring for other possibilities, we found a stone sarcophagus, parked outside the museum. 'It's an imitation of an Egyptian tomb,' Stephan said as we tried it out for size, late that night.

If Moses debriefed us afterwards, he did so in the name of Science. Devoutly interested in all perversion, he liked to quote Stekel, the author of a classic work on the psycho-pathology of sex. Indeed, as the prelude to a bout of furious fumbling, Stephan and I might have well spent the afternoon gossiping with him about a little-known aspect of fetishism or necrophilia. Knowing nothing about either would never have inhibited me from putting in my two cents worth. No topic did.

It pleased me to think that I counted for more than a mere female, and I struggled to keep up, going so far as to steal a primer called *Existentialism Made Easy* from the library. Its third-hand hint of profundity was more than enough. All I needed was a phrase of two, and by concentrating, for a moment, I could grasp just enough of any exchange to make fun of it. I was a natural, able to reduce the loftiest chit-chat to its lowest common denominator. It was how I kept up my end of the conversation.

Doubtless it was also camouflage of a sort. I had given up all hope of being mistaken for an alluring woman, only to find out that there were troubling limitations on what was, essentially, a comic role. Instead of being able to report on the exquisite tortures of love I was forced to dredge up the tawdry evidence, like the frangers on the floor of a stone tomb. Since this was as close as I came to plumbing the depths, I had decided that some dimension was missing, and after mulling it over in private, explained it to my own satisfaction. I was too normal, as far as I could see. It was a real handicap. Everyone knew that the most desirable women were bewitchingly neurotic, if not demented.

We revered madness. It is a sideline of the Romantic tradition which usually appeals to susceptible undergraduates, but in support of the contention that so-called insanity was a symptom of penetrating vision, we were less likely to quote Coleridge than our own modern authority, the psychiatrist R.D. Laing, who believed that the emotionally disturbed reacted to the pressures of family life with an instinctive logic.

What with Laing and the heavy-breathing histrionics of *The Alexandria Quartet*, we had convinced ourselves that the deranged were the true aristocrats of the empire of the senses; or, to put it another way, that there was something noble about giving in to the instinctual passions. The ramifications of this notion were to reverberate through the later 'sixties, a period which saw a great revival of the Romantic sensibility. It is difficult to disentangle the Romantic sensibility from the throes of late adolescence, and the people around me thought of themselves as outsiders probably assured of a tragic fate. I had no aptitude for tragedy, but I was willing to flirt with the idea of death. Perhaps not death, exactly, but something more along the lines of resurrection.

Though Stephan and I had engaged in overwrought discussions of our affair from the first, I was astonished when he stopped believing that this, in itself, constituted an interesting relationship. He talked about calling it quits, but it wasn't to be a clean break. I am slow to react to what your average thin-skinned heroine thinks of as educational experience. When it comes to the declension of love, every dawn is a new day, and I wake up more or less convinced that the man who ignored my wailing the night before will be ready to negotiate. Things did not work out that way, and before long we were caught up in a series of stormy scenes. I surprised myself in the middle of one drawn-out melodrama on the roof of the Fisher Library by pausing to consider if I were faking it, but it was hard to tell. The wind was whistling in my ears. I was sitting on the safety rail, balanced at a perilous angle, loudly accusing him of indifference.

While my behaviour became increasingly theatrical, Stephan managed to detach himself until he was unmoved by the most hysterical fuss. He got up and walked out of the beer garden of the Forest Lodge, after I scratched at my wrist with broken glass again. Or so he told me, when we talked about it not long ago. In the scene that he reconstructed, I fumbled around on the floor for ages, to find the cleanest sliver of broken glass. That may be so, because I am nothing if not fastidious. In fact, all that I am able to recall is that I was disgusted at the sight of the blood that welled up from a small cut, and having gone inside to wash if off, I asked the barman for a bandaid.

That was the finale, not long before the end of the academic year. I was sure that my life was over, but it gave me gloomy satisfaction to discover that I was losing weight, for once. With nothing better to do, I stayed home and studied. Perhaps there was no choice. My parents, who had returned from Europe only to hear rumours of our recalcitrance, kept Jules and me on a tight rein. I protested that I was broken-hearted, and was dragged along to the doctor in Dee Why, for a check-up. The pragmatic approach worked, in its way, and to my amazement I passed the examinations.

EIGHT

Frensham and the Six Day War

I was at Frensham, a fashionable, if decrepit, private school in a town on the edge of the southern tablelands, about eighty miles from Sydney. The outing, on a Sunday in December 1966, provided one revelation after another. Invited to stay for lunch, I found myself at the so-called High Table, on a platform at one end of the dining hall, rubbing elbows with an Anglican clergyman. I was still worrying about the small talk when, with a great scraping of chairs, teachers and schoolgirls alike leaped to their feet. Scrambling up in embarrassment, I kept my eyes fixed on my plate, and remembered having tea with the Turners back in Harbord. The same scoop of mashed potato. The same subservient beans. The same lamb chop, as dried out as the Nullabor Plain.

'For what we are about to receive,' intoned the pastor, 'may we be truly thankful.' Until that moment, I had been under the impression that grace was said only in nineteenth-century novels. 'Amen.' I had the job. 'Amen.'

During the interview, conducted before lunch in her office, the school principal, Mrs Sandberg, a rangy woman with cropped hair and an ill-fitting intimate manner, leaned forward to confide that she was also from Holland before asking if I still spoke Dutch.

'Yes,' I said, seeing no need to go into details. It was not a language one might have expected to find useful, in a school on the wrong side of the Great Dividing Range. 'We speak Dutch at home . . .' The rest of the interview did not take long. I said I could teach English and History. 'How many years of history did you do at university?' she asked. '. . . Oh, only one. I'm afraid that's not enough to teach. How many years of English?'

'Two,' I lied, and was immediately hired to teach English to the daughters of the gentry. Though I had been enrolled at the university long enough for the average student to pick up a degree, after the first year I had shifted the focus of my attention to the Piccolo Bar, a Kings Cross hangout for beatniks and drifters, going to so few classes in 1965 that it was only logical to skip the examinations and repeat. But Frensham did not appear to be exaggeratedly fussy about formal qualifications, and Mrs Sandberg also appointed none other than my friend Ina Klein, from Betar, who had dropped out of high school to become an art student.

It struck us as a bit odd that the two of us were to teach in a Christian institution, but we assumed that we had managed to impress the principal, who had gone so far as to make us housemistresses, all for the same forty dollars a week. In thinking it over later, I came to the conclusion that Mrs Sandberg picked me for an easy mark, and she put me in charge of 'West', the school's most ancient pile of perforated brick, where fifty-two girls slept in a dormitory half-sheltered from the elements by canvas blinds.

Behind this verandah was a long, dark corridor with tiny cubicles on either side, and on the first day of the school term, the following year, I waited at one end of the corridor to greet the people who stowed their progeny at Frensham. They seemed to arrive in a rush. A muscular blonde six-footer — the heiress to a concrete company fortune — galloped on in front, but her pals were close behind, dragging along their perfectly groomed sires and dams. I thought I heard hounds baying in the distance, but there was barely time to wonder what to do before the leader of the pack had reined in, as if we were separated by a stile. Tally-ho.

'Hello,' I bellowed so loudly that the nearest mothers winced, 'my name's Wynhausen, what's yours?' This unexpected opening forced me to play the scene like Margaret Rutherford, backing and filling as I trod on the toes of second-generation millionaires, braying as I peered upwards into their astonished faces.

The parents seldom came near me after that, perhaps because they wished to sustain certain illusions about the school. It had been founded by a pair of lively, Oxford-educated eccentrics who had progressive ideas about educating the second sex in an invigorating — indeed, freezing — environment comparable to an English public school. The vanguard of 1921 had been overtaken (even if the original chill remained), but Frensham's reputation still lured a few blue-bloods whose pedigrees conjured up images of thousands of acres and millions of sheep, images that in their turn conjured up actual pupils, from the parvenu families who are the bread and butter of an establishment trading on its association with the ruling class. Indeed, seen from the distance, that is to say, seen from the perspective of parents more preoccupied with the reputation of the school than the discomforts its regime imposed on students, Frensham may have looked just right.

The ivy-covered buildings, like the fine rose garden in front of West, filled out the picture of a fancy boarding school people carried around in their minds. Behind the playing fields, across the street from the main part of the school, was a creek lined with weeping willows. The surrounding countryside, reputed to be some of the most expensive grazing land in all Australia, served as a bucolic backdrop and even the town of Mittagong, less than a mile away, fitted into the picture by being quaint. The town had a doll-sized railway station with a white picket fence. The small cenotaph on a traffic island in the middle of the main street was done out with the usual dead flowers and inscribed with the usual Anglo-Celtic names, but the street itself was in transition, and shops that had only recently had faded floral wallpaper and flyblown baby bootees in the windows, had been taken over by matrons in tweed hacking jackets who sold pottery and Paddingtonia.

Changes of this nature were slow to make themselves felt at Frensham, perhaps because the attitudes to the town had faintly feudal undertones. Mittagong had been metaphorically adapted, to remind the WASPs of their place in life. Students (and teachers) referred to it as 'the village', in a tone suggesting that one might well expect to see the teenage gas jockey at the Shell station pull his forelock when a Mercedes full of Frensham girls whisked past, on one of the two weekends a term the parents came to take them out.

Some never came, and one was forced to conclude that they wished to preserve their peace of mind, by seeing as little as possible of the school, and even less of the people in charge of their children. Perhaps they were doing the right thing. Though Frensham is now very different, in those days only a clinician could have expected to meet so many neurotics in the one setting. The dormitory closest to West was run by an overwrought but haunted-looking character, who started conversations by apologizing, and then clutched one's arm, as if to cling to something substantial. She was terrified of men, loud noises, the principal and life in general. At night she drank, and was set upon by spectres. In a state of near-hysteria she would telephone, around midnight, to beg one of the housemistresses who lived nearby to chase the prowler supposedly lurking outside her window.

Within the confines of Frensham, this poor, lost creature could just manage to hold herself together, and she was not alone. The school's twittering Old Guard included up to a dozen teachers who could not have survived life on the outside, and whether or not it was the effect of institutionalization, between them they had so florid an array of tics and twitches that the staffroom at times resembled a sheltered workshop.

During the tense moments at the mid-morning meetings, one

sat waiting to see who would next dissolve into tears. No-one could have accused Mrs Sandberg of being a soothing presence. She would burst in on the scene, blowing into the room so that the door slammed, the teacups rattled, and one or other fragile pensioner dropped her milk arrowroot biscuits. In Mrs Sandberg's wake, one found oneself stifling the impulse to check if something had been left hanging, half-off its hinges. She was like a whirlwind which roils around without rhyme or reason, and that was on one of her good days, when she might well pause in the midst of a mad flight of words to enquire solicitously after someone cringing close by. On her bad days, there were rare, dangerous silences, and people tippy-toed past her lair, opposite the staffroom, where the teachers sat frozen in readiness for her entrance.

Quickly convinced that we would get as dotty as they were if we stayed in the school too long, Ina Klein and I had found a refuge of sorts in one of the sixth-form houses, a big, ramshackle cottage behind the creek. The housemistress, Lee, a weather-beaten American of about thirty, wandered about the place in hippie dress, tailed by her two fair-haired children.

They ran free, skylarking with the girls in the dormitory, or clambering over us as we sprawled in the long grass, luxuriating in Lee's company. In the 'States before her luck ran out, she told us, she had heard Bob Dylan at Newport and stayed stoned until she was back with the kids in California, where she heard him in concert again. Not knowing much as yet about the culture springing up around the music, Ina and I failed to divine the significance of the experience, let alone the fact that Lee, who was superstitious, considered herself to have lost the magic of being in the right place at the right time. That was not how it appeared to the people around her, because she had the knack of drawing them into her world, even if the world had shrunk to the bit of land behind the creek or the life around the table in her kitchen.

The sixth-formers were protective of Lee, but indulgent at

best about the limitations of other teachers who they treated with amused disdain. Condemned for the mousiness of our lives, we were judged to exist only in the realm of the school, much as servants used to exist in the realm below stairs, not that anyone would have put it so rudely. In organizing their own hierarchy, they were ruthless. A girl who arrived out of nowhere was sized up by a bunch of cold-eyed teenagers able to discern her financial status before she had so much as unpacked. Old money did not impress them, unless there was a lot of it being splashed about, for instance, on the parties that made the social pages.

Of course there were exceptions, and a code that few fourteen or fifteen year olds questioned openly was challenged by the rebellious girls in sixth-form, who liked to loll about voluptuously in the nude, pretending to take an interest in radical politics, or so I was assured long afterwards by a participant. The ringleader of the rebels was a tall, improbable redhead who was inclined to corrupt the morals of fourth-formers. Though she was subsequently to achieve fleeting fame as an assistant to Madam Lash, Sydney's Messalina of sado-masochism, she was not yet jaded in love.

Towards the end of the first term, the principal got wind of a misalliance between her and a skinny waif in West, and as one of the housemistresses involved, I was called in and ordered to snuff out improprieties; duly warned, I cantered down the corridor of West making as much noise as possible, in the hope of scaring off any couples pashing in the Prefect's Room. But Mrs Sandberg, who took her responsibilities more seriously, prowled around in the shadows with the senior mistress, presumably to catch the redhead in flagrante. I came upon the teachers by accident one night, and yelped in fright, because all that I saw at first were two tall, ghostly shapes, flattened against a wall by the stairs that led to my room. 'Shhh,' said Mrs Sandberg, as her accomplice slipped out of sight, if not out of mind.

The spirit of the school (a kind of Sapphic closet) had infected me after a month or two, and I conceived a pathologically-belated schoolgirl crush on Miss Ferris, the senior mistress, imagining her seated at the edge of my trestle-like bed, wiping my fevered brow. It was a reprise of a fantasy from my childhood, but the former phantoms had been males. Miss Ferris, in contrast, had a pudding basin haircut and a penetrating gaze. She was exceedingly tall, slightly stooped and generally stood with her hands clasped behind her back, like the Duke of Edinburgh on an outing. An intense Roman Catholic, who conveniently taught Latin, she was astringent in style and faintly condescending in manner. I could not bear to call her Beryl.

In first term, when I was still girlishly susceptible, I once shambled over to her in the staffroom. 'Miss Ferris, you have some soot on your forehead,' I said, trying to dab at it, before noticing that she was struggling to express a complicated emotion. It did not seem to be in character for her to declare her feelings towards me, right there, with everyone milling about before Mrs Sandberg crashed into the room, but I had my hopes. Ferris often had an expression of owlish surprise on her long, unlined face, and by now she looked positively astonished.

'It's Ash Wednesday,' she gasped at last. 'Is it?' I said obligingly, wondering what on earth she meant. But I had stopped reaching for her forehead.

I gave up trying to impress Miss Ferris. By the time the second term rolled around I had realized I wasn't going to impress anyone in charge, and could be as lackadaisical as I liked, at least in my domain. Once the winter was setting in, for instance, I saw little reason to patrol the house. The ambience of the West dormitory, on the top floor of a three-storey building with classrooms below, suggested that the girls were being prepared for all eternity. The place was cold as a tomb. In the evening, I dashed along the verandah to see if there was a girl in each bed (if only for the moment), switched off the lights, and left them to it.

The mornings were worse. One derived what comfort one

could from the clanking of the ancient heating pipes, trying to transform the sound into an illusion of warmth. The first bells of the day rang out at six, and while I crept deeper under the covers, wondering if the hot water would run out again, the hardier kids sprinted off to the showers in a barracks-like bathroom at the other end of the building. Though none of us had exchanged a word about it I had an understanding with the girls, who would come pounding on the door of my bedroom, a cell four feet wide. I was supposed to check on their toilette, and bending the rules a bit, often did so from my bed. In the half-light of the dawn, each girl filed past on her way to breakfast, stopping in the doorway to show me that she had bloomers under her tunic, garters on her stockings, and had artfully concealed whatever jewellery she insisted on wearing.

Once that was done and the place quiet, I had my own ritual, imagining the scene at breakfast before deciding if I dared skip it again. In the dining hall, at the ungodly hour of seven-fifteen, grace was said for clumps of oatmeal that stuck in one's throat. The girls bolted the stodge as if half-starved but that was over-doing it — they could have as much bread as they liked, and on the days it was still warm from the oven, some of the little idiots gobbled up to a loaf of it before going to the bathroom to make themselves throw up. Up at the High Table, meanwhile, the minor variations on a theme of gruel and Gravox were no more conducive to appetite than the social choices of the situation. Teachers new to the school conspired to avoid sitting beside the twitchers, the mumblers and the old lady whose jaws cricked like a starting pistol (none of whom would have dreamed of missing a meal), but it was hard to decide if it were worse to sit with one's back to the 300 girls down below, or to catch sight of them wolfing the food. I didn't have to worry about it, however. My friend Ina and I had arranged seating, on either side of Mrs Sandberg's father, who had arrived from Amsterdam for a longish visit. He was reputed to be a man of distinction: Mrs S. called him 'the Baron' even if he were in the room, but as a matter of fact, they were seldom in the same room, and that is where Ina and I came into the picture. It turned out we had been employed to talk to him.

Deathly-pale vegetables expired on our plates as we sat tensely deciphering the old man's proper Dutch. The trick was to keep him talking, but he paused to ask your opinion if your eyes so much as drifted across the table, and then the jig was up, because neither of us understood much of what he said. Still curled up in bed, I contemplated my empty seat next to his and stayed where I was, though rarely without wondering why Ina was so good-natured about being on duty from morning to night.

Breakfast was followed by Assembly, an occasion I also tried to avoid. The mood in the Assembly Hall conveyed the sense of suppressed hysteria that characterized much of what went on at Frensham then. The girls sat cross-legged on the cold floor, Mrs Sandberg made the announcements and then prizes might be given out to the achievers. The prizes were coloured girdles, with green girdles for hockey, yellow girdles for choir, purple girdles once in a blue moon, and as if all that were not precious enough, irises were occasionally given out to signify a still-higher plane of accomplishment. The girls were encouraged to react with feeling. They clapped frenziedly as the prizes were announced, a few burst into tears, and now and again a child in first- or second-year succumbed so completely to the atmosphere that she had to be dragged off to Sister to be pacified.

After the announcements, teachers and students alike bowed their heads in prayer. I had experimented a few times but it made me feel that I was knuckling under, and from then on, if I happened to be in the Hall during prayers, I stared straight ahead with my eyes wide open, like the murderer at the tennis match in *Strangers on a Train*. More often than not, however, I stayed away on religious grounds, an excuse that did double-duty. For the first, and presumably the last time in my life, I celebrated every Jewish holiday, generally by staying in bed with a good book. Being Jewish had rarely been so convenient, or, with the exception of a few days in June, so irrelevant.

In the first week of June, Ina and I drove pell-mell from Mittagong, going straight to her parents' flat in Coogee, where we met in secret with our old friends from Betar. Though a number of us had severed all connection with the movement, we were breathlessly caught up in the crisis of the moment. Israel, which had just been mobilized, was on the brink of war and even renegades like myself were more or less prepared to board the next flight to Tel Aviv. Ina, the one exception, was nevertheless involved. She was engaged to a student from Melbourne who was dithering about going, and had turned up to talk it over with her.

No-one else had experienced the slightest doubt. My brother's girlfriend, Eve, the English Rose, had already marched in to inform her history tutor at Sydney University that she wouldn't be around much longer because she had to go to war. Or course, there were one of two practical details to sort out first. People had been getting their passports in order, going to Nadel Studios for the passport pictures. Mr Nadel, the Cecil Beaton of Sydney's Jewish community, usually photographed the W.I.Z.O. princesses and the plump little princes whose coming-of-age rated a mention in the *Jewish Times*. My brother and his girlfriend had rushed to a rival studio, 'but they fucking rooked us,' said the English Rose, before we fell to arguing about how to get to Israel.

Our sense of urgency was typical. The consensus at the time was that the Arabs were about to make good on their old threat to drive the Jews into the sea. Jews everywhere had been galvanized into action, and at the very time that we met in Coogee, 5,000 people crammed into Sydney's Central Synagogue, already jammed to the rafters with cadres of Zionist youth who had marched through Bondi to protest against Arab aggression. The Arabs had not retreated, however, and at the synagogue the feverish appeal for funds was preceded by a gloomy assessment from a politician just back from a junket, who said things looked bad, but the Jews would fight to the end, as they had against the Romans at Massada.

Our 'war-council' in Coogee had started off on another note of defiance. In fact, the first skirmishes of the Six Day War seemed to be occurring in Sydney, where my brother and his pals from Betar had run up against a bureaucratic juggernaut more difficult to dislodge, as it turned out, than the Egyptian army. In short, Jules and Co. were engaged in a war of nerves with the satraps of the State Zionist Council, who claimed the right to act in the best interests of all Jews, and were being more swaggeringly self-important than ever. Outraged to hear that our boys had privately raised the cash to get themselves to Israel as volunteers, council officials had refused to give them the okay they needed to land. 'No sweat,' said Big Ed Adamek, who looked to be in full bloom, even if he insisted on lumbering around the room like a standover man in an Ealing comedy. 'We'll fly to Cyprus and hijack a fishing boat . . .'

In the end, the fracas with the council went on a day longer than the shindy in the Sinai. The Council's War Office was in the Maccabean Hall, and having moved into the room next door, the Betarim bivouacked there all week, taking turns to argue with officials and move the coloured pins on the map of Israel they had taped up.

I was to hear about both campaigns at long distance because by dawn, the morning after our meeting, I was navigating the craters of the Hume Highway, stopping only when the radiator boiled over, every half-hour or so. At Frensham, I brought my friends on the staff up to date. The love angle intrigued them more than the politics of the Middle East, and we gossiped enviously about Ina Klein, who had gone AWOL to stay in Sydney with her boyfriend. Unwilling to explain her absence to Mrs Sandberg, I lay low, but the girls were impossible to avoid.

'Is Miss Klein getting married, Miss Wynhausen?' someone in

3B bellowed in the middle of a poetry class. Marvell's coy mistress left them cold, too. 'What's he look like, Miss Wynhausen?' The question came from the kid whose father owned a concrete company. I had forgotten to banish her from the class as I usually did. It was some education they were getting at Frensham. I had only just found out, for instance, that the School Certificate exam included a section on grammar. Until then I had failed to teach it, airily informing my students that grammar was nothing but a set of dry-as-dust rules which inhibited literary licence. A little late in the day, I decided that the dullards had slightly more hope of parsing a sentence than of recognizing a single line of a Charles Lamb essay, and with that in mind I drilled them relentlessly, two or three times a week. They seemed to prefer it to poetry.

'What's his name . . . Whatsisname, is he really going to Israel, Miss Wynhausen?' The mysterious sources of their information suggested that my class could have taught the chaps at ASIS a trick of two. '. . . you going, Miss Wynhausen?' Whoever it was had sounded hopeful. 'Shuddup, all of you . . .' Saved by the bell, I went off to the local doctor, to have smallpox and cholera injections.

It amused him, for some reason, to be consulted about yellow fever. 'Oh, you're going to the Holy Land . . .' 'I'm Jewish,' I said, wondering why it always sounded like a non sequitur. 'You still don't have to worry about yellow fever,' he murmured, getting up to show me out, 'and, uh, good luck.'

The word from home was that my brother had run into a brick wall. Never sure whether the operators at the local exchange were listening in, I spoke to my mother in Dutch. 'Jules says I'm an old cow,' she informed me in English, sounding pleased with herself. ' "So I'm an old cow," I told him, "and you're still not going to Israel before you finish at university".'

'But you can't stop me from going,' I said. 'I'll be twenty-one in three weeks time.'

'I wouldn't think of it,' she said placidly.

When the news bulletin came on that evening, I was crouched over the small wireless in my study, feeling faintly ridiculous. The static on the line sounded like gunfire, but then, it always did. A BBC voice said, '. . . The Israeli Ministry of Defence has announced that the Egyptian armed forces launched an attack . . .' Static drowned him out. '. . . the Egyptian airforce has repulsed an act of uprovoked aggression by the Israelis, who have lost 432 planes . . .' Someone knocked on my door. 'Come in,' I screamed. '. . . three planes . . .' Kyrsty Macdonald, an engaging, harum-scarum fourth-year girl I liked, stood in the doorway with her friend, Rosalyn. 'If you're coming in, shut up for a minute. . .' I still had my head to the radio, as if listening for signs of life, but the bulletin was over.

'What's happened?'

'How would I know,' I snapped. 'I'm in bloody Mittagong . . .' It didn't make sense. The Israelis said the Egyptians attacked. The Eygptians said the Israelis attacked. The Egyptians were lying, of course. 'You two want coffee?' Perking up immediately, they chorused, 'yes, please,' and smiled, conspiratorially. On a cold night, I put a little cheap brandy in each cup. How many planes in an airforce? Mum was right not to let Jules go. He'd get his silly head blown off. 'The war in Israel's started. This morning, I think.' Stuck in Mittagong with a car likely to conk out for good on the next trip over the Razorback, just as Israel was being wiped off the map.

'Are you going to go?'

'Don't ask me, Kyrsty . . . the way the Mini's going I won't even get to Picton.'

Back with news from the front the following afternoon, Ina Klein reported in a tone of derision that her sister had joined the would-be soldiers at the Maccabean Hall, while my brother, who had sulkily given up the idea of stowing aboard a freighter to Cyprus, was muttering about leaving home. 'I can't believe the way they're all carrying on,' said Ina. A stranger had rushed up to ask if she were going to Israel. 'You must be joking,' she told him. Hundreds of people had flocked to the hall, the previous evening, with individuals who had not had anything to do with the Jewish community bursting in to volunteer their services. 'No-one knew what to do with them, except ask for a donation. That sobered 'em up,' said Ina, who had always been a pragmatist. But for one thing, she would have been unnervingly detached from the mood of the moment. 'So what's happening with your boyfriend?' I asked. '3B wants to know.'

Since he had gone back to Melbourne, he also missed out on the fun. The Betar contingent camped out in the hall had been told that only people with medical qualifications were wanted in Israel. 'No sweat,' said Big Ed, and made some calls, before sloping off to pick up three nicely-forged truck drivers' licences. When three of our boys, including Ed, flew out the following week, the report about it in the *Sydney Jewish News* mentioned that they were ambulance drivers.

But by then it was all over. A couple of days into the war, it had emerged that Israel had scored the decisive blow right at the start. The Egyptian airforce pilots had been ready for an attack at dawn, and when it didn't happen, they left their planes and went in for breakfast. 'Listen to this, Ina,' I said, flapping a day-old copy of the *Sydney Morning Herald* at her, and explaining once again that the Israelis had bombed hundreds of the Egyptian planes on the ground, having flown in an arc over the Mediterranean and come in unexpectedly from the north. It was fantastic. Unable to get enough of it, I tracked the Israeli advances on an atlas in the school library. For the one and only time in my life, I identified wholeheartedly with the cause.

'So you didn't get there, after all,' said the doctor in Mittagong. It took me a minute to figure it out. The war had been over for weeks, and my fervour had faded into memory. 'No, I didn't. Some of my friends went, after the war, and they're stuck in this kibbutz out in the desert, getting up about three in the morning to pick apricots . . .' The doctor had started doodling on the pad in front of him. 'Of course, that's not what I came about,' I said, deciding to plunge in. 'I'm twenty-one, today. Can I have a prescription for the Pill?' He was an urbane, humorous man, but he looked up in amazement, and I may have misinterpreted his expression. 'Just in case.' That time, he laughed out loud.

'It's easy for him to laugh,' I said to Ina, after we escaped from the 'soiree' someone had insisted on organizing for my birthday, 'and you too, even if Whatsisname's in Melbourne. But I'm gonna end up like the rest of them here.' Doubtless confused about cause and effect, we were sure that anyone who stayed in the school would turn to the bottle or her own sex for consolation, not least because Frensham had little to offer in the way of heterosexual temptation. The men with whom you could imagine exchanging more than a word or two gave lessons but played no other part in the life of the school. The exception was a music teacher, who was blind. The girls liked to say he played organ in the dark. Though he had a wife, she did not figure in the stories they made up about him. Someone had seen the French teacher lying on the carpet in the music room, with her feet up on a stool. It was in broad daylight, with the windows open, but that did not inhibit the little dears from inventing an adulterous liaison, because they said things like that about every man around the place, including the bluff fellow who ran the Frensham farm. Oddly enough, there was one old lecher, a gardener who stood around leaning on his rake, leering at the young ladies as they hurled themselves around the hockey field, and was reputed to have availed himself of the favours a few of the senior girls thrust at him insistently.

'There's always the Baron,' said Ina. 'I thought you liked older men . . .'

This was a reference to one of my more disastrous attempts to get laid. I went to Sydney as often as I dared, rattling along the Hume Highway again and again, until its blind corners and scarred stop signs were inextricable from the sparse, fumbled pleasures and frustrations of my weekend forays. A fortnight or

so in the company of jittery women did more than set one's teeth
on edge, and I would start off the journey in so ruttish a mood
that I fantasized about picking up a hitchhiker and going at it
there and then, in the back seat of the Mini. I lost my nerve at
·the last moment, which was just as well: the only guy I ever
stopped to give a lift to was a moron missing a front tooth whose
spit hit the dashboard when he spoke. Though it should have
taught me something about a series of escapades doomed to
absurdity, I continued to have more than the usual trouble in
reconciling desire and the necessary denouement. It tended to
make me capricious at the wrong moment.

Towards the end of first term, a stocky, square-jawed, prematurely balding man, a pharmacist out of his element in the Piccolo Bar, had taken me to his mother's house at Darling Point.
A pair of Pekingese slavered around his feet. He was looking
after them while his mother was away, he said, creeping around
in his socks as if we might be sprung by a servant who had got
her dates mixed up. I could tell that it bothered him that I kept
peeking under the dustsheets on the spindly antiques. His ma,
the dowager, must have been loaded, because there was a painting by Degas somewhere and he had paused in front of it with
a dumb, worshipful look and proceeded to give a little lecture
about it. The muttering in the background convinced him at
long last to get on with it, but I had registered the fact that my
ardour was cooling rapidly.

He had to be persuaded to turn the asthmatic dogs out of the
bedroom. 'They always sleep here,' he said anxiously, lapsing
into silence until we had undressed and stretched out when he
suddenly thought to ask if I were on the Pill. 'Nope.' I was
laconic about it, but he leaped up as if he had been bitten, started
rummaging around and went on searching in some other room.
I stayed where I was for a minute, wondering why a pharmacist,
of all people, would have so much trouble finding a condom,
but by the time he reappeared I was dressed, more or less, and
I bolted, my brassiere still dangling from my hand as I skittered

down the driveway and up the hill to the Mini.

Undaunted by experience, I kept going to Sydney every other weekend, if only to install myself in the Piccolo Bar with Ania, my closest friend. Ania, whose working-class Jewish family had fled Poland when she was in her teens, worked as a waitress. Though resolutely uneducated, she was shrewd, outspoken and quick to get to the heart of things by puncturing pretension; gossiping with her after a fortnight at Frensham gave me a sense of getting my feet back on the ground. But the school's Old Guard managed to make it clear that I was flouting some unwritten rule. They were timorous about it, of course, slowly working the conversation at the High Table around to something that had happened at school over the weekend, and raising their eyebrows over the astounding revelation that I had missed all the fun. I decided to brazen it out, and in an exercise of logic, absented myself from the High Table as well.

I expected to be carpeted at any minute, but the summons did not come until the third term. I imagined Mrs Sandberg would have something to say about my disappearing trick, but no, it wasn't that. Frensham skimped on auxiliary staff by appointing unsuspecting novices as part-time clerks. I was supposed to make the school's travel arrangements, which meant booking the train tickets at the end of term, and sorting out the schedules of the solitary travellers who went off for family funerals or visits to the orthodontist. Not known before or since for attention to administrative detail, I found it all too easy to lose a girl and I spent a couple of mornings a week hanging around Mittagong railway station to see if the latest stray had turned up. I didn't mind. It was my alibi for skipping Assembly.

No-one had gone missing for more than a day or two, and all considered, Mrs S. was overdoing it. I burst into tears but she liked scenes too much to give over. She was used to browbeating the frail old things who would have done anything to stay at Frensham, and having realized as much, I managed to stop snuffling and threatened to resign. She backed off a bit, saying that we would try to work things out. Doubtless she was being realistic — it was difficult to replace a teacher in third term. I didn't pull my socks up but the fifteen-minute scene in Sandberg's office taught me more than anything else all year, and thinking it over, I resolved to stand up to people in a position to give me orders. I had felt powerless at first and I was determined not to let it happen again. Within a day or two, I had decided to go back to university the following year. If I were qualified, I reasoned, I could tell the boss to stick it.

NINE
Our Crowd

Though I had severed most of my connections with the tribe, on one occasion, in 1968, I found myself surrounded by its elders. It was my brother's doing. He was marrying the English Rose, whose father was not only a rabbi, but the bossiest man we had ever met. One immediate result was that the wedding could not have been more traditional — our families went to war, and Manischewitz supplied the so-called wine.

The guests were already gossiping in the squat little synagogue on the outskirts of Sydney's western suburbs when hostilities broke out in the kitchen of the house next door. 'You're wearing Homburgs and that's all there is to it,' the rabbi shouted. 'I'm not,' his future son-in-law said mildly enough to get under anyone's skin. Jules, who looked unnatural in a suit, kept fingering the collar of the perfectly-fitted shirt, as if he might choke to death at any moment. He remembered looking down on a surge of Homburgs when he was a nine-year-old choirboy at the Great Synogogue in downtown Sydney, where manufacturers whose grandfathers had been pedlars in Bialystock acted like English gentlemen. 'No way.'

'We can't,' said the rabbi's son, Ian, who had hidden the hats on the chairs tucked under the kitchen table. 'They've disappeared. I've looked everywhere, even in shul.' At seventeen, Ian towered over his father. He seemed to be about to pat him consolingly on the top of his head, or perhaps to swipe the kippah and hide that as well. 'It's time, dad. We'll have to go without them.'

The rabbi thumped the table, something fell over, and his wife crept in, looking helpless. She would have liked to finish fixing her corsage and wig, but did not dare. 'Harold . . .'

'This,' said the rabbi melodramatically, 'is easily the worst day of my life.'

They relented, of course. It was his day. In the first of his starring roles he strutted down the short aisle, with Eve on his arm, his eyes sternly fixed on the Homburgs up ahead, and with a two-step of ceremonial gravity, he popped up under the Chuppah and waited for silence. Though it was a cool day in June, the synagogue was stifling. Swathed in a bridesmaid's dress in dark-green velvet, I stared sidelong at the front pews, inspecting the boiled faces under hair lacquered in place, until I caught my mother's eye. She winked. Ordinary Jews used to caper for joy at an affair like this. If you couldn't have a Rothschild in the family, a rabbi was the next-best thing. But we thought it was a nuisance. Harold was a conceited little fellow so used to having his own way at home that he tried to bully us as well. Every single word he had said about the wedding emphasized that it was his show, from beginning to end. He had telephoned often, in recent weeks, and he only had to say, 'Harold, here . . .' for my mother to start giggling. I winked back.

Now he was saying something about a 'fifty-fifty partnership in marriage' and one or two of the guests looked downright sceptical, as if he were going against the grain. Not that Harold had got off scot-free. Though his wife was anxious, apologetic and devout about the least of his needs, his daughter could match him for intransigence down to the final bitter words as she fled into marriage at the age of twenty, unable to stand one more interminable Saturday afternoon out in the dreariest of suburbs. Harold couldn't stop himself from mentioning it, either, when he alluded to the lucky couple at long last. 'In fact, there's plenty of room for improvement . . .' Cathy, the other bridesmaid, glanced at me in alarm. She was not Jewish, and Eve had forgotten to warn her that no occasion was too exalted to wash a bit of dirty linen in public. The rabbi was restrained, however, allowing only that the lovebirds still had a thing or two to learn about good manners towards their parents.

He had claimed that he had to invite about three-quarters of his congregation and half the rabbinate. It left our side with a reduced guest list, which was just as well. They might not have said so, but Aunty Nan and her friends considered themselves a cut above the Jews who lived on the edge of civilization (an hour's drive from the Cosmopolitan in Double Bay), and who probably went to the sort of shul where no-one noticed if you wore a cardigan.

Not even our nearest and dearest had bothered to fake much pleasure at the prospect of driving out to the sticks to hear Harold's nasal East End intonations, before driving back, pell-mell, for the festivities in a hall in Woollahra. The balloons looked a little limp by the time that we reached the place, and the classy gardenias in the floral arrangements reeked of stale perfume, but these were details lost in the crisis of the moment.

Though he presided over a shul where people were sometimes to be seen in white twinsets, even on Yom Kippur, highest of the High Fashion Days, Harold had managed to turn the tables, socially speaking. Nevertheless, he seemed surprised that my mother objected to a seating plan which had her guests at the two tables at the back of the hall, with the Betarim. For a minute, she was speechless with rage, and then she spluttered, 'Chutzpah, Harold, what chutzpah . . .' seizing handfuls of the place cards, as if to redistribute them. The argument continued out the back, in the kitchen, where Mrs Goodkind, the caterer, was supervising the preparation of the usual boiled chicken. Referees were called in, the English Rose burst into tears and mum threatened a walkout, but by then it was all over bar the shouting, and my aunts, uncles and honorary relations roughed it with the rowdies down the back. I could hardly believe their luck.

The bridesmaids were at the High Table, and I was with the geriatrics. On my right was a venerable great-aunt of Eve's who spoke only Yiddish. On my left was the Chief Rabbi of Sydney. Our conversation was strained, after the opening gambit. I had started to light a cigarette. 'Not before the toast to the Queen,' he hissed, closing his hand over mine like a vise. I played at being deaf, but it was boring. 'Do you speak Yiddish, Dr Porush?' He looked startled.

'Why do you ask, my child?'

'Oh, this lady here doesn't speak English.'

They conversed, and I leaned forward politely, scanning the room to see it there was a single person I could have considered screwing. Porush resumed his position and toyed with the gefilte fish. I decided not to ask if he liked it. The last time I had criti-cized the taste of gefilte fish, a friend of my aunt's called me an anti-Semite. Still and all, people ate it because they were Jewish, and I had no intention of touching mine.

Harold, the Master of Ceremonies, had grabbed the micro-phone by his plate to introduce himself, with a modest chuckle, as the father of the bride, before explaining that this was only an introduction because we would be hearing from him later in the afternoon. 'Of course, you've all met my wife, Yetta,' he said, 'and as you are undoubtedly aware, we are especially honoured by the presence of the Honorable Dr Israel Porush . . .' I stole a glance at Porush, dipping his heavy old head to a scatter of subservient applause.

Harold was a lightweight, but Porush had this way of looking into the middle distance, and I couldn't help conjecturing about his hotline to a God I didn't believe in. 'I beg your pardon?' Jesus, he was asking where I went to synagogue. Talk about tactless. 'My parents are with Cremorne shul,' I said carefully, 'but I live in Balmain. It's nice, Balmain, near the old wharves, almost European, with those winding little streets . . .'

'Yes, I know.' He smiled encouragingly, and turned to the per-son on his other side. What did I tell him about Balmain being

European for? No-one said that except my mother, who was dismayed by it.

'Balmain,' she had snapped, in the last act of the drama played out on the day I said I was leaving home, 'who ever heard of Balmain?' It had happened in the summer, a couple of weeks after I left Frensham. The man who had taken me out came in for a drink and that woke dad, who started patrolling the hallway in his pyjamas. Since nothing was going on, I was in a frenzy of outraged virtue. I dropped the bombshell at breakfast the following morning, getting the whole thing off on just the right footing, by announcing furiously, 'I'll never have to eat liver for breakfast again . . .'

My mother acted as if there had been a death in the family, wailing that decent Jewish girls did not run away from home unless they had something to hide. 'I'm pregnant,' I said, 'can't you tell? It happened last night when dad left us alone for eight-and-a-half minutes.'

'Don't speak to your mother like that.'

'Like what? Mind your own business.'

'If you speak to your father like that again, you can get out of this house . . .' Before long, she was considering the shame of it all. What would she tell the family? She could just hear people talking about it at B'nai B'rith. Only in moments of stress did she resort to such arguments; fortunately she was herself again by the time we went off to inspect the terrace house in East Balmain.

In fact, she was rather quiet, and Tante Ali did most of the talking. I had dragged Ali along because she was known for her modern outlook on life, but even she paled a little at the sight of the grey stucco slapped over the exterior of the dark, narrow-fronted house. The real estate agent, Balmain impresario Reggie Window, seemed to overreact to the presence of a pair of Dutch matrons, because he kept tapping at things to show that the house wouldn't fall down. Someone else was moving into the attic, but the second-floor bedroom in the front had a varnished wood floor, an improbable plaster rosette in the ceiling, and iron-lace on a balcony which hung slightly askew. If you stood on tiptoe, you could see the inner harbour. 'All these bedrooms for only twenty-five dollars a week,' I said excitedly.

Depressed or not, my mother couldn't tolerate this soft-headed enthusiasm, and she quizzed the agent about the plumbing and the gas, as she ran her hand over one dusty surface after another. 'You'll never keep this place clean.' It was her only triumph. All I could see was the patina of age, and I was thrilled. As a child, I had begged her to move us into an inner-city tenement, like the sooty relics with washing strung between them that you saw from the trains pulling out of Central Railway. 'But mum, this place was built in 1887 . . .'

'I know,' she said flatly, 'I saw plenty of houses like this in Arnhem before the war. Creaking stairs, cracked cement and weeds instead of a garden . . . dust everywhere, not a flicker of daylight, creeping damp . . .'

'It's rising damp and you're exaggerating.'

'I've seen it all before,' she said, 'it's like a ghetto around here.'

Eve's great-aunt was tugging at my elbow. She had lapped up the tinned fruit salad, and seemed to be jiggling her shoulders in time to the music. 'Herbie Marks Trio,' she said in impeccable English.

'I know.' The band reminded me of any number of functions at which I danced with my father, or with the son of some friends of the family, a boy who was several years my junior. When I was fourteen, the top of his head came to my nose.

'You dance,' she said.

Everyone else was having a high old time. My brother's friends had moved some tables and were dancing. They must have tapped a stash of hooch. All I had got my hands on was kosher wine, and kosher wine is the Jewish answer to holy water — you could drown in it without getting drunk. Did Porush really say that anyone could dance? The old guard was ganging up on me, and even mum and dad were out on the floor, doing the foxtrot, while I sat there submerged in self-pity, pulling petals out of a manufactured-looking carnation.

'Your sister-in-law looks lovely,' Porush said.

'I think they're going to sing.'

Jules had lost the struggle for the microphone, and Harold announced that he had a special treat for us, a return engagement by the Bridal Couple and their friend, Henry Berkovic, who was back from Eretz Yisroel where he had gone as a volunteer. In its heyday, two years earlier, the trio had materialized at parties in the Hakoah Club or the Maccabean Hall, often to the surprise of the guests, who seemed to be expecting the likes of Daniel Barenboim instead of a few straggly-looking folk singers in duffel coats. It wasn't the trio's fault. Their gigs were arranged by a guy who had some connection with conservative Jewish causes, and had taken up culture, imposing himself on the three of them as a manager. Once, when they refused to perform at a United Israel Appeal affair, for twenty-five dollars all up, their manager said, 'So forget it. If you don't want to sing, I can get Maria Callas, just by picking up the phone . . .'

'Mum's got the best voice,' I told Porush, who had asked about the family, 'and when she was young — well, nineteen or twenty — in Holland, she was asked to join a radio show, to sing, but her father wouldn't let her because singers were supposed to be loose, um, loose women.' I couldn't believe I had said it to a rabbi, 'you know, like actresses.' My mother used to sing when she was cleaning the house. I had grown up listening to the songs of Charles Trenet, orchestrated only by a vacuum cleaner. 'My brother has a good voice as well. That's why we were in your choir . . .'

The trio was huddled around the mike. Jules strummed an

experimental chord on his guitar. His eyes were half-shut, and as usual, he looked to be in an existential stupor, dark suit or no dark suit. '. . . I sing flat,' I whispered, only because I hated leaving it up in the air. Getting the crowd-pleaser in early, the trio had launched into 'To Life, To Life, L'chaim'. Someone important had heard them singing at a gala at the Chevron Hotel, and in no time at all, they were asked to sing 'To Life, To Life, with Orlon' for an Israel Fashion Week at David Jones. The number had been choreographed and rehearsed before it emerged that they had to join Actors' Equity. David Jones declined to spring for the union dues, amazingly enough, and my brother, who is nothing if not obstinate, called the whole thing off.

Out the back, in Mrs Goodkind's domain, the sound of breaking glass was followed by an ominous thud. Some of the Betarim were paralytic. Harold stayed at his post. So did I. Down below, almost everyone had joined hands to circle the room, because the trio was finishing off with 'Hava Nagila'. Now and again, Dr Porush gazed at me with patriarchal reproach, as if he had somehow divined that I had strayed. Until the previous week, in fact, I had been involved with a creep whose occupation as a truck driver for Coca Cola should have made the first of mum's questions about him redundant.

'No, sorry, he's not Jewish,' I had tried to be polite, 'but it's okay, I'm not going to marry him, or anything.' For once I regretted having issued the usual gazette on my love life. 'He's all right, really. I met him at the Piccolo.' She had not looked reassured. The crowd of drifters and layabouts in the tiny Kings Cross coffee shop where I still hung out included a handful of foreigners who were always saying they were about to leave, because Sydney was too provincial. Of course we encouraged all criticism, grateful to them for taking an interest. 'He's from Montreal. Says he doesn't like it here.' He was as mysterious about his past as a remittance man, though I had not found anything of note when I went through the things in the old shoebox hidden in his closet. The only relics of his former life were a few cards, an old photograph of a woman in black holding a baby, a note from his mother, who could barely string a sentence together, a Canadian Mounties badge, and a 'Dear Harry' letter from a girl in Sweden.

I had gone through the shoebox a fortnight after moving into his bed-sitting room in Kings Cross. With mum barely recovered from the affront of my leaving home, I thought it best not to mention that I was living in sin in the red-light district. 'What can I tell you? He's just a normal person.'

I was exaggerating. The first night that we went out he had carried on like a madman, screaming abuse at the motorists on William Street, because his bike had been pinched while we were in Lorenzini's. With several of the cops out the back, roughing up a pair of drunken sailors, we had waited for ages at Darlinghurst Police Station. He stalked about in a frenzy. 'Busy place, hey,' I said loudly, after the desk sergeant waved him away for the third time.

'How old are you, lass?' the cop had hardly bothered to lean forward, and the menace was subliminal, but Harry was magnificent. He told the son-of-a-bitch to leave me alone, and got us thrown out of there in two minutes flat.

'It's all your fault,' he said bitterly, as we legged it past the 'Rm to Let' signs in Victoria Street.

'What d'you mean, my fault? He told you to get your registration papers, that's all. If you'd taken the hint about the bribe, you'd probably have the frigging bike back by now . . .'

'Fuck it,' said Harry, and he kicked at a harmless mongrel pissing on a plane tree. 'I'm not going back there.'

Suppressing certain doubts about his sanity, I had moved in within the month, though I kept the room in Balmain. No-one had asked me to live with him before. No-one had pulled a carving knife on me in the middle of a domestic, either. 'Normal people don't spend every night in the Piccolo Bar,' my mother had said, and dad gave her a glance of admiration.

I couldn't stand it for another second. 'Excuse me,' I muttered to no-one in particular. The great-aunt had disappeared. Porush, who was deep in conversation with another rabbi, looked relieved to be talking shop.

'Do you want to dance?' said a friend of my brother's I hadn't seen in years.

I was aggrieved. 'I don't care. I've been up there two hours with the rabbis interrogating me about where I go to shul, and there wasn't even any booze, except that disgusting sweet wine . . .'

'Listen, he's going to make a speech!'

'Bullshit, Jules never made a speech in his life!'

I was wrong. Harold had just announced that his son-in-law had the floor. 'Only Harold could take five minutes to introduce someone else's speech. What a pain in the arse . . .'

'Shhhh.'

'Do you know that people have been telling me to shut up all my life . . .'

'Shhhh.'

My brother finally looked as if he meant business. He tapped the mike, straightened up, and stared over our way. 'Thank you,' he said, and walked away.

TEN
Headlong Hall

That winter was as depressing a time as any I remember. I was
sharing a dump full of broken-down furniture with one girl who
couldn't stop crying and another who was never home. The dark
old house was filled with whispery sounds. The walls sighed, the
stairs creaked of their own accord and the windowpanes rattled
in the lightest wind. I left the lights on all day but there was
nothing to see. The furniture downstairs must have come from
the Salvation Army. The sofa in the dusty little parlour at the
front had springs protruding through fabric which was green
with age. The gaudy travel posters taped to the wall in the dining
room were as outlandish as fancy dress on a skeleton. I lingered
only in the kitchen, liking the starkness of the rough, white-
washed walls and the bricked-up fireplace.

Like it or not, throughout 1968 I had it all to myself until Jan
came home from school, changed into a floral brunchcoat and
reappeared, her hair in curlers and her swollen features set in the
look of determination which meant she was on another diet.
Though secretive, she had confided in me a couple of times and
I lived in dread of it happening again, after she showed me the
contents of the chest usually kept locked in her room in the attic.
I was aghast. The thing belonged in a museum, like a scale-
model of the original Hills Hoist, or Johnny O'Keefe's padded
jockstrap. It was a hope chest, full of carefully folded and
refolded linens, strata even the untrained eye could read back to
the bedrock of 1956, when someone had started off the

collection with two Namatjira tea-towels.

I had said something polite, trying not to think of the lacy black underwear she left draped over the shower-rail. Not only was Jan a traditionalist, she acted as if her role model was Veronica in the Betty and Archie comics. 'That must be my date,' she would trill from the second-floor landing if a bloke turned up to take her out, 'can you tell him I'll be there in a minute . . .' Her behaviour grated on me, and my behaviour grated on her. 'I wish you wouldn't leave the lights on all the time,' she called out, coming into the kitchen late one afternoon. Her voice was loud enough to be heard at the back of the classroom, and I made another mental note not to go into teaching. I was back at university, with a scholarship and pocket money from the government, the reward for indenturing myself, rather doubtfully, to the Education Department.

'They weren't on all the time,' I said, averting my gaze because Jan had started painting her toenails, there and then. 'I've been out fighting the pigs . . .'

I had reached the Front Lawn just as students were lining up for the march, and with no pressing engagements for the afternoon I had drifted along, in the middle of a thicket of Che Guevara posters. There must have been about a thousand students straggling down George Street. Stern young Trotskyists in red headbands nipped at our heels, but no-one took much notice: the ranks had thinned here, bunched together there and spilled over the footpath, for a quick argument with a man who was wailing, '. . . go to Russia, you'll be locked up, go to Russia . . .'

Hundreds of police were waiting near the entance of the railway station at Town Hall, but it was the motorcycle cops in their glossy black boots who stood out. They were dark-jowled and menacing. Seeing them, students started seething about Askin, the premier, who was reputed to tell the police when to rough up the demonstrators. 'One, two, three, four, we don't want your fucking war . . .' Much as I liked protest for its own sake, the sense of camaraderie came and went, and I had deserted my comrades at Chifley Square after catching sight of a hippie who was hauling out the usual props of agit-prop, with a high hat for Uncle Sam and conical hats for the innocent North Vietnamese in their black pee-jays. The anti-war plays were all the same. The very prospect made me feel disdainful of the mob. 'There were cops all over the place, thousands of 'em, champing at the bit.' The old policeman who had heard me murmuring, 'we don't want your fucking war' had grinned and told me to wash my mouth out with soap. 'They only made eight arrests. It was a great march, though.'

'That's what Robyn said about the march last week . . .' Robyn, the social worker who shared the house with us, was usually self-effacing but could be headstrong: in the autumn, she had taken a couple of handicapped children from an institution to watch an anti-war rally, and almost lost her job after a tiny, ten-year-old moppet in callipers appeared in a picture in a magazine, obligingly waving the orange and blue flag of the National Liberation Front. 'But I still can't see what difference it'll make if either of you get arrested.'

'You sound like my mother.'

'I think I like the pink better,' said Jan, wriggling her toes.

'No, the red's okay. I thought you told me red was supposed to be such a turn-on they wouldn't let you wear it at Teachers' College.' That seemed to satisfy her, but I was left wondering where she had got the idea that I wanted to be thrown in gaol. I ambled down George Street with the troublemakers now and again, but on the day the revolution came, I was sure to be lounging around at home, waiting for something to happen.

If nothing else, the affair with the Canadian madman had liberated me from the workforce. I had dabbled in the stockmarket as he did (because it gave us something to talk about aside from ice hockey scores) and my conscience hadn't prompted me yet to expunge my $900 stake in the filthy capitalist system. I called my stockbroker occasionally and I dropped into a few lectures at the university, a schedule that left a lot of time to kill.

The weeks dragged by: every day was a life sentence of unwanted solitude. I was condemned to sit staring morosely at the flecked linoleum stuck to the top of my desk, contemplating the emptiness of existence in unrhymed lines which tailed off well before the end of the first stanza. Though Robyn was seldom home before midnight, she turned up out of the blue one evening in September and I was downstairs in an instant, yapping around her like a terrier trying to round up a single, slow-moving sheep.

'You look different,' I said. 'It must be your hair.' Her long, blond hair had been plaited and coiled, demurely, at the nape of her neck. 'It's great, it looks . . . it looks like you're in the Swiss Family Robinson.'

'I found out about the Valium,' she said firmly, 'it's addictive.'

'I know. I asked the chemist. But if she doesn't take it, she cries all the time.' Jan, who was in a bad way, dragged herself home from school only to hide out in the attic, where she had rifled the contents of the hope chest, to sob ceaselessly into Broderie Anglaise pillowcases.

'There's other ways to treat depression.'

'Depression? Is that all it is?' I didn't know the word could encompass so much despair. 'Did you tell her?'

'I've been telling her for ages that she ought to see someone about it.'

'Oh,' I said meekly, deferring to the professional tone, even as I imagined Jan stretched out on her bed, more swollen-faced than ever. If I went up to her room to see what I could do, it was only to mumble platitudes and gingerly stroke her hair.

'I haven't talked to you for months,' I had trailed Robyn into the kitchen, 'are things okay with John?'

'We're getting engaged . . .'

'Mazeltov.'

'I beg your pardon?'

Mr Right was a sandy-haired, mousy musician who had managed to turn a slight stammer into a major impediment to conversation. He often looked distracted, as if listening to chords in his head, and no wonder. Not long after they crept into the house, Robyn was sure to be in the middle of a drawn-out aria. Every note was audible in my room next door: in recent weeks it had been as close as I came to having a sex life of my own.

'You're amazing, I couldn't have waited to say I was getting married. No, don't make me coffee. Someone told me they put soapy stuff in the powder to make it dissolve and now I can taste it all the time . . .'

'Look, uh, would you mind not saying anything to John yet?'

'You're the original blushing bride, Rob.' Going pink like that probably meant you had more libido. 'Did he give you a ring?' I tried to blot out the image of the plaster rosette around the light fixture in her bedroom. The whole thing had plummeted down one night while they were at it, stopping short just above the foot of the bed, because the electrical cord held. What on earth were you meant to say about engagement rings?

'Not yet. We're going into the city on Saturday.'

It was strange how getting engaged made people smug, as if they had pulled off a religious stunt, rising to a higher plane of existence. 'Gee, that's great. What kind are you going to get? If you're Jewish you have to get one of those knuckle-dusters, with gold prongs and a diamond this big. That's what it says in the Torah. In Hebrew . . .'

It had taken her a while to get it straight about the language: early on, she had asked politely if we always spoke Jewish at home. 'Anyway, I saw this lovely little ring in a shop up the other end of Darling Street.' I paused in confusion. It was in a pawnshop. 'But I can't remember which shop, now.'

'That's all right. We saw one ages ago in Prouds, and John put it on lay-by.'

'What did your mother say?' The old lady was always making

trouble because John was a Roman Catholic.

'I'm not going to tell her about it. Not yet, anyway.' Having just sat down, Robyn was back on her feet, hovering again. 'What about you?'

'No-one's asked me to marry them, that's for sure. Mum says I'm wasting my life, sitting around doodling.' How could you get engaged without telling your mother about it?

'I thought you were writing poetry . . .'

It was my own fault — as usual, I had announced the plan well in advance of the actual production. 'I thought of doing this series called *Anywhere but here*,' I said, making it up that moment, 'but I haven't really got very far yet.'

The line which had popped into my head, sounding particularly poetic, was 'It snowed that year', but I waited in vain for the next burst of inspiration. All my efforts to do up some scenery with 'twisted limbs', 'bare, crackling twigs' and 'frozen tears' had been unavailing, and I had asked myself more than once whether I was cut out for the literary life.

Upstairs in my room, I took a fresh sheet of paper, wrote, 'It snowed that year', stared at it for the longest time and then, with great deliberation, added a semi-colon, nodded appreciatively and awarded myself a Marlborough, before writing to Nestlé, to inform the company that I did not like the taste of Nescafé, any longer.

At the end of the year, I met the outriders of the Sydney 'Push', who were lecturing at a summer school in Newport, where they arrived with a raffish-looking clique which included other academics, disaffected teachers and several seedy optimists struggling to make a living as film critics. Intellectuals who mocked themselves almost as freely as they mocked each other, they were irreverent and, in private conversations, ribald. In the mornings they wandered around in a haze, recovering from hangovers, in the evenings they were as disreputable as the circumstances allowed, and in between they managed to cope with the self-taught eccentrics involved with the Workers' Educational Association. In the diverse, if dogged, crowd of students were a few old-timers who followed their own train of thought and spoke up regardless of what was going on in the class. A reference to Joyce's Dublin, for instance, would tempt some sexagenarian to ramble on about the way things were in the country town he could recall, brick by brick, from his childhood. It amused the lecturers, who must have been accustomed to the pace of adult education. One of them hummed under his breath while waiting for his turn to talk; another kept nodding briskly, as if affected by a tic; and a third, W.E.A. tutor Don Anderson, a paunchy, gentle man with a mournful air, paused in an attitude of profound thoughtfulness at every interruption. The technique was to stand him in good stead long afterwards when I was at him about something, but by then he and I were married.

It wasn't love at first sight. He half-remembered a glimpse of me limping around in a broken Dr Scholl's sandal, and I remembered seeing him and his friends looking thoroughly undesirable, around dawn, on the first of January, 1969. About ten of the people who had caroused through the night had washed up by the rock pool at Whale Beach, where the men stood shivering, waiting for one of us girls to dive in. They were pathetic. Bleary-eyed, sallow-skinned and flabby, several of them were in the woolly-looking trunks that only Englishmen on holidays in the tropics are meant to wear, and they glanced at each other sheepishly, as a couple of sun-bronzed lifesavers trotted past, muscles rippling. Don Anderson winced, buttoned up the shirt he had just unbuttoned, and said he needed a beer.

'The trouble with you is you're too sensitive,' said Michael Thornhill, a tall, gangling man who spoke out of the side of his mouth, like Jimmy Stewart in *Destry Rides Again*.

'Sensitive, hell,' said Don, staring with distaste at the sunrise, 'it's all this fresh air . . .'

By the time I clambered out of the pool they were dressed and in a huddle against the cliff, speculating if it were worth driving the twenty miles to the early-opener at Pyrmont, by the docks just west of the city. 'Are they really going?' I asked one of the women. I had heard about a pub at Pyrmont where Aboriginal girls were raffled, like chooks, though perhaps not on the dawn shift. 'Of course not,' she said disgustedly, 'they just like talking about it.'

Back in the city, I was determined to hook up with them, and did so by a process of fits and starts, but looking back now it almost seems as if my life changed overnight. To see them again, I had to run the gauntlet at the Newcastle Hotel on George Street, around the corner from the quay. The hotel, which was done out half-heartedly in Edwardian style, with dark wood fix-tures and fake gaslights gathering dust, had been a haunt of low-lifes and artists since the 'forties. In due course it was adopted by the Libertarians, the inner circle of 'the Push'.

The Libertarians were famous for believing in Free Love, and by the 'fifties, wayward students were following them around. With little else in Sydney in the way of a bohemian subculture, 'the Push' had come to include academics, artists and writers, as well as dissenters of every stripe, many of whom met at the New-castle on Friday nights.

The place, packed out before dark, could be daunting at first, and after waiting in an open doorway hoping to see a familiar face, I tried to talk to the three women standing near me on the footpath. 'Slumming, are we?' one said, staring at me as if I were something nasty under a microscope.

'Well, uh, I don't really know anyone here . . .'

'Can't you find somebody else you don't know?' The speaker, who appeared to be in her early twenties, tossed her long, blonde hair around as a sign of contempt. Lighting one cigarette after another, she sucked on them with theatrical intensity, like a scarlet woman in a B-grade movie, but I wasn't game to send her up and her cat and mouse game went on until one of her friends was bored enough to ask who wanted a beer.

The ritual was mild considering that the women could be savage for no reason, except that it was expected of them, as it is expected of a native policeman in a white-run colony, persecuting his own kind to keep his place in the pecking order. Until the nineteen-seventies, the woman were outsiders who did not think to complain about it because 'the Push' gave them an alternative to the stifling conformity and narrow-mindedness of suburbia. They shared in the excitement of flaunting their freedom as they mapped out what was said to be another arrangement between the sexes, but even so, the prospect of being a stray fuck palled if it were more or less the only formal role you were permitted to play, and the casualty rate was high. Someone later counted up to find that ten of the women suicided and two were murdered. The survivors cut themselves up so often that no-one looked twice at a bandaged wrist.

But from my perspective, the scene at the Newcastle could have conjured up the goings-on at any suburban pub. The men, who appeared to prefer each other's company, stood around talking about the prospects in the races at Randwick the following day. Mystified by their behaviour, I assumed that they were nostalgic about the life they had left behind. Why else would a bunch of bohemians imitate the style of the average working stiff?

Fortunately, the style was less in evidence among the literati like Frank Moorhouse, a writer whose first collection of stories was published later that year. Moorhouse was the standard-bearer of a division of 'the Push' identified with Balmain. I had met him and his cronies at the summer school, and before long, I drifted into a desultory sort of affair with Ken Quinnell, arguably the seediest of them all. He looked decadent, as if he slept in until the afternoon. His pale, freckled skin was almost transparent and his hair was prematurely grey, images difficult to relate to the burst of staccato laughter which followed everything he said. Though Quinnell never breathed a word about horse-racing, his interests were on the speculative side, and he and Moorhouse were about to launch an underground newspaper called *uphill*, which may have lasted for four or five issues. I figured as a patron of this lost cause, because Quinnell had commandeered the dining room of my house to spread out his effects, including piles of yellowing newspaper, the flotsam and jetsam of his other sorties into underground publishing. If he appeared at a civilized hour, it was to work on a dummied-up copy of *uphill* laid over the dining room table. He had installed himself for good as far as I could tell, and our affair ended without inconveniencing him, because he took up with Sandra Levy, who had moved in the week before.

Sandra and I had met at the Newcastle, joked about being Jewish and dismissed it as an irrelevance, although she complained about looking the part. People were always sidling over at bus stops to ask her where she was from. She has a mass of coal-black hair and a long, expressive face, a juxtaposition which used to make some of the natives uneasy. Thin as a rail, she dressed in exuberant, clashing colours. I admired her style tremendously; everything about myself seemed to pale in contrast, even if I was out the front, telling people to check their hats and coats at the door.

By the time that Sandra moved in, Headlong Hall had turned into a hostel for waifs and strays, with so many people tracking in and out that some of the more casual callers had trouble remembering where they were meant to sleep. Sandra's husband, a filmmaker, came visiting at odd hours, dressed in fireman's boots and a red fireman's helmet. His life was arranged according to the impulse of the moment. If he started thinking about his marriage at three in the morning he turned up, but instead of pressing his claim in the usual way, he would creep upstairs, wake Quinnell, and try to lure him to a house in a neighbouring suburb where he claimed to have stowed a couple of nymphets. 'Don't tell San,' he would whisper, urgently enough to wake the dead.

It was a rare night without incident. I was in bed with some-one, an Englishman, when a guy neither of us knew burst in, stared at us suspiciously and demanded to know the time. He came back twice to make sure that it wasn't two o'clock yet.

'I can't stand it,' said the Englishman, waking me up all over again to say he couldn't get any sleep, but his behaviour was not so normal either. He had once arrived unannounced, by shinnying up the drainpipe and coming into the bedroom from the first floor balcony, perhaps the only sign he gave of being anxious to see me.

If the nights at Headlong Hall were unpredictable, the days were far from dull. Towards the middle of the year, when Quinnell and Thornhill were working on a movie, they asked if they could film a scene at my place. They were vague about the nature of the scene, though Thornhill said they weren't having any of that arthouse shit, and Quinnell might have gone so far as to say that it was something of an experiment. Unwilling to be an unpaid clapper girl, I demanded a credit and left them to it.

'It got a little out of hand,' Thornhill said cautiously, when I came back from university around nightfall and asked how it had gone. 'Do you want a beer?'

'You know I don't drink beer. Where's Ken?'

'I'm out here, tidying up,' he called out, sounding muffled, as if he were trying to disguise his voice.

'Tidying up what, for fuck sake?' The small room, behind the kitchen, had nothing it it but an ancient bath and a top-of-the-line world war two icebox.

'It did get a little out of hand,' Thornhill said again. I dodged past him and stood staring. The white-washed walls were black, the bath was coated in soot and even the cracked linoleum was charred.

'I thought there was supposed to be a murder scene, after the rape.' I was determined to be sophisticated about it. My voice wobbled with the effort.

'There's an explosion after the murder, but we might have

used a bit too much petrol.'

'Well, you could have said you wanted to use the place to blow it up.' I guess I should have been grateful. Some years later, Quinnell accidentally burned down the back half of the house he was in, and he wasn't even making a film.

'We'll clean it up,' he said smearing a bit more soot around the bath, 'after we get back from the pub. Sandra said she'd meet us there . . .'

The Forth & Clyde hotel in Balmain was the focus of our social life. The pub was at street level, in an old two-storey building with overhanging balconies and wide double-doors along two sides, a layout which allowed you to duck in without being bailed up by a posse of libertarian women and duck out again before one of the Balmain layabouts sidled up to ask for a loan. Several scenes merged at the Forth & Clyde, the local for the contingent from 'the Push' as well as some of the campus radicals. In the course of one of the Springbok protests, the radicals had dropped black dye into a swimming pool a few miles off and fled to the hotel, where two of them were arrested. The dozens of people who swarmed into the police station managed to get them released, and they were carried back to the bar in a victory procession.

Though every other night seemed to spill over into a party, these occasions were merely dress rehearsals for the spree on Saturday, when Balmain lawyer Murray Sime, our impresario, would make the rounds, greeting people like a politician on the make and pausing to tell fifty or sixty of his intimates around the bar the address of the party.

It was unwise to restrict invitations to a party because Sime had his scouts out, and like as not, the crowd from the Forth & Clyde turned up anyway, brandishing half-empty flagons as if they were bouquets and trampling on the sensibilities of the official guests — subdued anthropologists in flapping sandals and academic wives who would have preferred to think of Balmain as Bloomsbury — civilized people huddled together like sheep in a storm while the rabble made itself at home. Ravaged poets materialized from a cloud of marihuana smoke to rave about Rimbaud; student radicals lunged at the art, seizing on Balinese shadow puppets and fat little fertility symbols for a sermon on the spoils of imperialism; the layabouts finished off the Glenfiddich they found stashed in a restored pine dresser in the kitchen before one of them expansively propositioned the hostess; and, as if all this were not enough, Sime's sidekick, Adrian Heber, had meanwhile cornered a couple of official guests and was claiming to be a professor of Oriental Studies, or a defrocked archbishop or, as happened once, a dog. On that occasion, he was down on all fours, barking, and the person who remonstrated with him was promptly bitten on the ankle.

I should have known better than to give a party for the people my mother had pigeonholed, one and all, as 'your new friends'. 'I know your new friends are very sophisticated,' she said when I phoned to discuss the menu, 'but I'm sure they would like some Dutch roast beef . . .'

'I don't want to overdo it. Everyone else just spreads something on Jatz crackers.' Of course I did want to overdo it, without going so far as to round up the crowd from the Forth & Clyde, to take them to the pictures and back home for icecream cake. Imagine giving a party people talked about afterwards instead of boasting about their hangovers. I could conjure it up. The rooms downstairs were bathed in glowing light. People were deep in conversation about the future of literature. Seeming to be everywhere and nowhere, I flitted about effortlessly, making things happen. 'I'll get some salami,' I said. 'It's not so exaggerated.' Offended, my mother told me not to forget the Jatz crackers.

Quinnell looked pleased with himself. 'Remember when Wilding got into your room by climbing up the drainpipe?' I paused, with the plate still in my hand. I had been picking broken glass out of the savouries, a last-ditch effort to maintain the tone of my party. 'Five minutes ago, someone left that way . . .'

'I don't believe it,' I said, feeling abused. Things had gone wrong from the start, when someone accused me of being bourgeois because I tried to bar a couple of the Balmain layabouts.

The tally for the evening included a fistfight, two broken romances and a friendship that was hovering in the balance. Frank Moorhouse, who could be at his most engaging at a party, had decided there and then that he was being persecuted by Michael Wilding, another writer. The two of them were always making wild claims to keep the atmosphere sufficiently charged. Not knowing much about it, I assumed that it inspired them to dramatize their rivalry. They liked to write stories which played off each other's neuroses and it gave them more than enough scope. 'He's been trying to find out what I'm working on.'

'Why don't you hire a private detective and really freak him out.' It was an act of charity to give a paranoid something definite to go on. 'Catch him spying on you, like he used to spy on me. Coming round here Saturday mornings . . .'

'Did you see *Southerly?*' Don Anderson said, looking embarrassed. Emotional excess always seemed to take him by surprise, and the next half hour must have been heavy-going, because he was plastered by the time I saw him again, coming round the corner from the kitchen with an unopened beer in each hand. Quinnell was still telling me about the fracas upstairs. 'I knew I shouldn't have let the bastard through the door,' I said angrily. 'He wasn't here five minutes before he put the hard word on the mad woman in the attic, and now he's in my bed with someone else.'

'Not now he isn't . . .'

'I hope he broke every bone in his body.'

'Taking a high moral tone, are we?' said Don. The nicest people were disappointing guests. But I had no illusions about Quinnell. 'Is that for me?' He helped himself to a beer. 'No, it's not,' Don said very distinctly, and staring in suprise at the can left in his hand, he swayed a little, dropped into the old armchair parked under the stairs and passed out cold. I was sure he hadn't said so much as a word all night about the future of literature.

The bodies lying around were gone by morning. I came down-stairs to find Quinnell tossing empties into a carton which was leaking. 'What's wrong with you?' He never cleaned up. The back bathroom still looked as it had right after they blew it up. 'I mean who are you trying to impress?' At least he had the grace to leer. Sandra had gone back to her husband and Helen Scott, who I'd seen on and off since we were at school together, had meanwhile left her husband and moved in the previous month. Without an excuse to barge into the house Quinnell had pined for a bit, or so it seemed, because he disappeared for a few days before he came back to court Helen. He had worked harder at it than was usual with him, once appearing, almost shamefacedly, with a bunch of scraggly-looking violets. Helen, to her credit, had said that violets made her think of death. Still, judging by his presence, he had managed to storm the Bastille and there he was with a different woman, back in the same old room. 'You're unbelievable, Ken ...' I couldn't wait to tell people about it. 'Really. No-one will believe it.'

'You get used to a bed,' he said.

'Not the men I meet ...' Though the Englishman continued to call in from time to time to badger me with questions about my alleged infidelities, the affair was over. I was still moping when Don Anderson asked me out, to visit a friend who lived in the country.

'I'll probably die in a car crash,' I said to Helen Scott, and we passed the time until Don turned up debating if the St Christopher medal in her ex's ute would have protected a Jew. 'Probably not,' said Helen. 'It never protected me, and my mother taught Sunday school. On the way back, just sit close enough to grab the wheel.'

Cautious in some respects, Don drove with ill-advised

bravado when he'd had a few beers. The first time we went home together, after a party, he had climbed into the station wagon, backed it straight into a telegraph pole and scowling, as if no automobile was going to get the better of him, pressed his foot on the accelerator so suddenly that we slammed forward into another lightpole. 'University car,' he muttered, as if that explained everything.

'Does that mean you need a degree to drive it?' I had complimented myself on my daring; after all, I hardly knew him, and his silences were heavy enough to be intimidating if, like me, you spent a lot of time agonizing about being intellectually inadequate.

Six months later on the day we drove out to Windsor, I sat in his car, the same station wagon with a crumpled fender, wondering how on earth to get him talking. It was hard not to feel that silence was one's own fault. 'Are you all right?'

'Oh, yes,' I said ardently, 'I really like being in the country.' The paddocks were yellow. The livestock looked half-starved, as usual. 'But you must be sick of it. Someone said you were in Gundagai last week, doing a seminar on James Joyce.' If my father had come along for the ride, he would have told Don about the first time we saw the Dog on the Tuckerbox, and my mother would have added that she preferred it to those boring old war memorials with the English names. Arbuckle, Brown, Campion, Curtis, Davidson . . . We were never stuck for conversation. The only trouble was it didn't go very far.

'I was in Wagga,' he said gently. So much for that.

'Tell me about *Ulysses*.' Surely that was good for a long trip.

Don sighed deeply. 'I'm on holidays,' he said.

ELEVEN
The Office Radical

I lack a spiritual dimension. To my way of thinking, public prot-
estations of faith are in poor taste, and anything that smacks of
mystical experience is on a par with extra-sensory spoon-
bending. But I was once the victim of a short-lived conversion.
I was a reporter on the *Bulletin* by then. Long associated with
reactionary opinion, the magazine had been dragged into the
twentieth century by its editor, Donald Horne. Protest movements that the *Bulletin* would have dismissed out of hand a few
years before were reported at least as sensibly as they were
reported in the *Sydney Morning Herald*. But I was surprised
when Horne agreed to let me write about the drop-outs
rumoured to be up north, near Cairns in Queensland.

'Waddya want to go up there for, love?' said the police con-
stable in Cairns I asked for directions. 'We can tell you all about
the hippies.' He did so at length in language which revealed that
the revolution hadn't reached Cairns as yet. Only his directions
were vague. It was two hours before I found the disorderly
sprawl of tents and humpies, hidden in the rain forest outside
Kuranda, some twenty miles north of Cairns, off the road
snaking along the top of the cliffs beside the turquoise sea.

Moments later I went native, stripping down to my car keys
to dive into a freshwater pool fringed with gigantic tropical
ferns. Not only was it disconcerting squatting down stark naked
to explain my presence to the drop-outs sunbaking on the rocks,
I had to convince a number of them that I wasn't an official in

disguise. But with the introductions over, the rhythm of life in the commune quickly proved agreeable. Expected back within the week, I cabled from the post office of sleepy Kuranda to say that I was continuing my investigation of the counter culture. I had stayed a fortnight before I heard about the lice; there and then I fled to civilization.

It was obvious that I was a changed woman. I rolled my own cigarettes and went to work barefooted. Horne affected not to notice for a bit before he asked, with exaggerated civility, if I wanted to borrow the sandshoes Hollywood reporter Charles Higham had left in a filing cabinet in the office. I grumbled about it only to hide my disillusionment with the alternative lifestyle.

One of the flower children, a heroin addict who called herself Sunshine, had arrived unannounced to stay at Headlong Hall. For close to two years I had shared the house with Don Anderson, a man of otherwise famous tolerance, who would mumble something like 'get back to Nirvana . . .' at the very sight of a person in an embroidered shirt and a beaded headband. He was irritated by the soothing manner I had brought back from North Queensland, and he very nearly moved out on the evening that our guest, the junkie, told him that red meat makes you aggressive.

Sunshine disappeared instead, along with my Arpege perfume and my natural bristle hairbrush, these evidently having been bartered for the embroidered Indian shirt she left behind. 'That'll teach you to promote a cause,' said Don, coming home in high good humour because I'd telephoned to tell him the coast was clear.

'I know. I wish I'd put the nits in the story.'

He didn't say anything for a minute. Before I knew him well, I assumed his silences meant he was deep in thought, when all he was doing was polishing a line. 'You could write it again,' he said slowly, 'and call it "The Other Side of Paradise".'

I had started out in journalism as a cadet on the *Daily Telegraph*. Opportunities were opening up for women, previously condemned to an apprenticeship on the social pages, where they made the tea and ran errands for the editor. Though the other newspapers had loosened up a fraction, so one might find the occasional murmur of protest in a publication as stodgy as the *Sydney Morning Herald*, the *Telegraph* stood firm against the tide. The proprietor, Sir Frank Packer, was a larger-than-life larrikin whose idea of a tease was an editorial suggesting that police in the 'States start shooting at the blacks rioting in the ghettos. The *Telegraph's* coverage of the local scene was faintly more restrained, but political protest effective enough, for instance, to block the traffic, was bound to be depicted as '. . . mob rule . . .'

Considering the paper's reputation, I was in for a shock. On my first day at work, in March 1970, I barged into the Chief of Staff's office to tell him that there were anti-censorship demonstrators outside the Gala cinema, a couple of blocks away. With no more than a cursory glance in my direction, he suggested that I investigate the cause of the fuss.

'Me?' I said on a rising note, my astonishment giving way to panic as I cast around for a way to add that the demonstrators were my pals in 'the Push', the organizers of an anti-censorship campaign in which I was marginally involved. They hoped to provoke the authorities and succeeded beyond all expectation, after a Libertarian faction led by Wendy Bacon turned *Tharunka*, the student paper at the University of New South Wales, into an underground newspaper which carried enough erotica to attract a shower of criminal charges. Merely publishing and distributing the paper became an act of defiance conservatives interpreted as a challenge to the system. Though the politicians couldn't stifle dissent, they could silence its rudest voice, and they resorted to the law to drive the newspaper out of existence. The editors were charged with no fewer than forty-one counts of obscenity and indecency. Briefly imprisoned for refusing to answer the questions put to her in court, Wendy Bacon stretched her week in the cells into countless articles analyzing the experience. For the moment, however, she was outside the Gala cinema, along with Sandra Levy and Michael Thornhill, who had just bet I couldn't get a reporter from the *Telegraph* to stroll over to talk to them. 'Me?'

'Why not?' said the Chief of Staff, advising me to double-check the spelling of people's names, as if that were all a novice needed to know. The story appeared almost as I wrote it, except that a sub-editor had censored the phrase, 'fuck all censorship'. I was still celebrating my debut in print when I found myself in a glass cage across the aisle from the Chief of Staff's glass cage, checking the times that the sun set, the moon rose and the tides ebbed.

Cadet reporters were assigned to the so-called shipping round to bring them down a peg, but strictly speaking, that was overdoing it. The atmosphere at the *Telegraph* was on the fusty side. Reporters worked in the murky gloom of a large room which may have been lit by a single, yellowish bulb. The dust of the ages appeared to have settled on the sub-editor's table, where crusty characters in green eyeshades sat bent over the slips of copy as if they had not twitched a muscle since the Relief of Mafeking. I was wary of them, however, having been dressed down at full volume by an ancient who summoned me from halfway across the room by shouting: 'Hey girlie, you there in the trousers . . .'

Being blooded on the job was all very well, but after six weeks in 'shipping', I protested that I was bored. The sequel was sheer farce. Within a day or two, word had filtered down that I was to be the *Telegraph's* film critic, standing in for Billie Burke, a raffish old lady with dyed black hair and rouged cheeks, who had vivid memories of the introduction of the talkies. Miss Burke had been mugged, and until she recuperated I was to write under her by-line.

I was filled with wonder that someone would pay you to go to the pictures in the afternoon. Pay me, of all people! Unlike the echt Billie Burke, I had 20-20 vision, but that was my only qualification as a reviewer. It didn't teach me a great deal, as no less a judge than Frank Packer was later to remark, but I loved it. Going to work day in, day out, gave me a sense of belonging. I had drifted about for years, unsure what to make of myself, and I couldn't have been more exhilarated at stumbling into something that seemed to resolve the question once and for all.

'I'm a reporter,' I'd say if I ran into someone from university, trying to sound nonchalant, even if I knew what was coming next. In my circle, it could be embarrassing to admit that one worked for the *Telegraph*, an institution identified with the ultra-right. Student rebels had raided the place, after an anti-war demo, to complain that they had been libelled as pinkos. Undoubtedly entertained, Packer offered to donate $10,000 so the students could pay a lawyer to sue him for libel.

Though I had taken anti-establishment politics for granted, that was now out of the question: in the *Telegraph* building, on the corner of Park and Castlereagh Streets, I felt as if I had been dropped behind enemy lines. Not quite sure what to do about it, I launched surprise attacks on the old men writing editorials in favour of the war in Vietnam. The poet Kenneth Slessor, and several other leader writers who were likewise grey and withered, had offices across the corridor from mine. 'I thought this might interest you,' I would say, pressing an anti-war pamphlet on one or other of them, before I fled. They were too astonished to argue, and I was left to have it out with another of my neighbours, a columnist by the name of Margan, who would come back from a long lunch and take it out on the copyboys, until I strolled into his office to make trouble.

'I see you've got your Veet Cong pyjamas on,' he would say, smiling thinly, but within ten minutes he was sure to be shouting that I ought to go to Russia if I liked the Reds so much. Warned off, after plastering his office with gummy anti-war stickers, I stuck them over his typewriter, a vintage Remington for which he had an inexplicable fondness. Not long afterwards I was called in to see the Chief of Staff who asked me, rather wearily, not to wear an anti-war badge to the office. I did as I was told, and waited a week or two before broadcasting the fact that I had become the 'media organizer' for the Vietnam Moratorium Committee.

My role as the office radical seemed to have little effect on my career at the *Telegraph*. Instead of reviewing films I had graduated, so to speak, to writing about television for 'Leisure and Pleasure', the entertainment guide published in the Sunday edition. I was apprenticed to an engaging pair of cynics who took everything in their stride. Not only was the television coverage regulated, but at least two-thirds of the column inches were devoted to praise of Channel Nine, Packer's station in Sydney. Our sharpest barbs were aimed at Channel Seven, then the only other commercial channel, and every so often we were expected to remind readers that the ABC was run by a bunch of velveteened highbrows who were out to lunch.

Now and again we dared each other to hint that a program on Channel Nine was a shade less diverting than, say, *Gone with the Wind*. A sub-editor was sure to kill the story at the last moment. But the system did fail once. I wrote a review disparaging a new horror series on the boss's favourite channel, and against all odds, it appeared in print. Embarrassing as it now is to admit, the opening line was: 'This show will not be everybody's cup of blood . . .'

The day after it ran I was summoned by Kerry Packer, the old man's second son. Ita Buttrose, who edited our pages, was already in his office. Though Buttrose was known as something of a martinet — able to reduce a rebellious copygirl to tears in two minutes flat — she took no part in the surreal exchange which followed, but sat in silence, her face a mask. I glanced instead at Packer, and quickly looked away. He was a rough cast of his father, but where the old man might have been carved out of stone, Kerry Packer's features were unfinished and rubbery. There wasn't much time to mull it over. He had started shouting the moment I walked in, and berated me for five minutes before I understood the substance of his allegations.

'You didn't even see it,' he yelled, stabbing a thick finger at the *Sunday Telegraph* opened to my review. The publicist had refused to let me see the program beforehand. I wrote about it anyway and when the shit hit the fan, he told Kerry Packer's brother, Clyde, who ran the station, that I hadn't seen the show. 'Of course I saw it,' I said in amazement, 'and so did everybody else. It was on television last week.'

Packer stared at me suspiciously, but telephoned his brother at Channel Nine. 'She says she saw it,' he bellowed, by way of preamble. The two of them immediately had a very heated argument about my viewing habits. 'How would you know what she saw,' Kerry Packer finally roared into the telephone, 'you weren't fucking the girl, were you?' QED. Mortified at his forgetting that there was a lady present, I peeped sidelong at the impeccable Ita Buttrose. Her eyes were still cast down demurely. 'You better watch it, Elisabeth,' Packer said menacingly, the instant he had hung up. 'You better watch yourself. Blood's thicker than water, you know.'

Instead of being sacked, I was graded as a reporter, ahead of schedule. Native ability had nothing to so with it; native cunning did. Cadets had to pass a shorthand test before they were graded, and I had gone to the trouble of winning over the shorthand teacher, a squat, beetle-browed woman with vague social pretensions. She thought it was beneath her dignity to negotiate with the sharp-featured kids from the western suburbs who had talked their way into the *Telegraph*, at that time the only morning newspaper in Sydney where you could get a cadetship without acting as if you had been to prep. school. They were held back. 'And you,' Miss Whatsername said coyly, as if she were about to ruffle my hair, 'you passed the test . . .'

I was keen, if not much else, and in August 1971, Donald Horne agreed to give me a job on the *Bulletin*, doubtless because I was in the right place at the right time, having raced upstairs to see him about three minutes after I heard that another reporter was leaving.

Horne was said to be an irascible editor who tore up people's copy and chucked it out of the window. Something of the sort had happened once, he told me long afterwards, but having ripped up a dummy of a magazine called *Weekend* he was to edit for Packer, he ran downstairs and dodged in and out of the traffic on Elizabeth Street to retrieve the scraps of paper. Though he had mellowed by the early 'seventies, he still managed moments of inspired unpredictability. If the atmosphere at a Monday morning editorial conference was sullen, probably because he had just bullied someone, he might launch into an imitation of Arthur Calwell — the right old ratbag who led the Labor Party to defeat after defeat — or stretch himself out on his desk, to swivel around on his backside, shouting, '. . . this is what I mean by horizontal layout . . .'

He insisted on celebrating Anzac Day at the New Hellas restaurant, in sight of the war memorial in Hyde Park, and with the rest of us throwing nervous glances at the old diggers who had struggled over to the Hellas for their one day of the year, he would clamber up on a chair to embarrass us into silence before he gave a satirical speech.

The Hellas was the favourite watering-hole of Sydney's literati. The crowd at lunch on Fridays included writers, reporters and people from the Forth & Clyde starting to make a thin living as reviewers and freelance editors. The would-be filmmakers darted from table to table, to maintain the pretence that they were expected elsewhere. Horne presided over the *Bulletin* table in the corner and Richard Hall, a former reporter who was then an adviser to ALP leader, Gough Whitlam, was in shouting distance, at a table with Don Anderson and Frank Moorhouse.

Though I rode in on their coat-tails, it didn't inhibit my

slightly smug pride at being acknowledged as part of the scene. Without knowing where I was going, I had arrived where I wanted to be. Reporters are prey to the illusion that they are close to the heart of things, and people from one sphere of my life kept turning up in the other. Moorhouse was a columnist on the *Bulletin* and Don, then a tutor at Sydney University, doubled up as the magazine's television reviewer. If they joined the *Bulletin* table, late in the afternoon, Horne couldn't be coaxed to leave until long after the waiters had lifted the chairs on to the tables all around us. Somehow it was always left to the women to break up the party and to try to drag him past the P & O bar, where the stragglers from the Hellas were nervously eyeing the bright, noisy flock of office girls at the other end of the counter.

'We promised to go back, Donald,' Sandra Forbes, the magazine's literary editor would say as she and I trotted alongside him, like sheepdogs. But it didn't make much difference. Fridays were complicated by the fact that the *Bulletin* went to press the following morning. If our lunch had gone on long enough, by the time it was discovered that some copy from Canberra had been mangled in transcription, Horne would storm around the office, threatening to sack the chief sub. I once intervened. Horne stared at me in absolute astonishment, and stormed off in the opposite direction, muttering to himself.

I had convinced myself that I was one of his favourites, though there was no evidence for it, and I spent hours and hours hanging around on street corners, or in the entrances of the city's arcades, ready to pounce on passers-by for the 'vox pop' which might, with luck, reappear as a quoted phrase or two in one of his political essays. I was irrepressible, the only requirement for legwork like that. The way I looked at it, the only strain in our relations was his refusal to increase my pittance, about $100 a week, after tax. Unable to get a rise out of him by threatening to see Packer, I made an appointment, late in 1972, and rashly bearded the old lion in his den.

Intent on setting an egalitarian tone, I marched into his office determinedly, as if at the head of a phalanx of D-grade reporters, and tried to reach over to shake his hand. With an acre of desk between us, I very nearly somersaulted into his lap. Packer was old and sick by then. His stony features were eroding, and his spectacles were as thick as Venetian glass. None of it was the slightest consolation.

'Well, young lady,' he boomed, 'what have you got to say for yourself?' Thoroughly unnerved, I stammered out an an account of my two-and-a-half years with his company. I forced myself to linger over the cover stories that I had written for the *Bulletin*, but he just stared, sitting motionless, until I had run out of steam. '"Leisure and Pleasure" never taught anyone anything,' he snapped, and that was that.

It was just as well. Five more minutes with Packer and I would have confessed that I was willing to work for nothing until after the election. The struggle between the reactionaries and the reformers was going on in the *Bulletin* itself. Horne not only toned down the copy from the Canberra correspondents, who were moss-backed conservatives, but let the rest of us loose on the campaign trail.

Towards the end of the campaign, I was sent to follow Doug Anthony, then leader of the antediluvian Country Party, around the wilds of Queensland. He and his confederates were tipped to lose. Nothing could have been sweeter than to stick like a burr to his side, as Anthony flew from Lismore to Rockhampton to Bundaberg, to rally the party faithful wedged into school chairs set up in higgeldy-piggeldy rows in one or other local hall.

The women, tightly-permed, were in mail-order crimplene. The leathery men came over all sly with a young woman from the city. They were farmers and small-town shopkeepers who might have been painted, poignantly, clinging to traditions which were dying out. But I saw them one and all as a remnant of the 'fifties, a reminder of the Australia I couldn't wait to leave behind. They made me nervous. Of course it was irrational, a relic of some ancient fear that my mother and father would be defenceless against them. They were the people who couldn't hear what you said because you had an accent; the people who told you to go back where you came from if you didn't fit right in, and if they didn't like foreigners, they liked Jews even less.

Perhaps I was imagining it. In my hearing, they talked of nothing but the Yellow Peril.

Bundaberg was on the last leg of the trip, and by then we were in the one electorate in the nation where the so-called Liberals were giving their preferences to the National Socialists rather than the Labor Party. In the town hall, a troglodyte by the name of Crawford called for a strict White Australia policy. Crawford had convinced himself that hordes of Chinese had sneaked into Western Australia, '. . . and they're coming here,' he told me, immediately after the meeting. I couldn't keep my eyes off his tie-pin, an opal cow on an opal boomerang, and I glanced up just in time to see Doug Anthony backing away. It was the very image to contrast to my first image of him behind the scenes, back in his office in Lismore.

'Incidentally,' he had said, after talking for ten minutes to the reporters who were to travel with him, 'this is my wife'. She stood next to him, and he finally turned to face her ten minutes later to ask, 'love, can you get me those ties and shirts?' I couldn't wait to use it in my story. The asides seemed to reveal more of his character than anything in the official script. Of course it all depended on your perspective. People who thought it perfectly natural for the little missus to fill in as a valet would wonder why I had bothered to report it. People who bridled at his use of the word 'incidentally . . .' would see him as I had, at that moment, in all the fervour of his smugness.

But his side was outflanked, at last. Our side was seized with a sense of anticipation which kept resolving itself into small victories against the diehards. People were fighting for rights that only rebels and dissidents had talked about a year or two before.

In a battle in which I participated, women laid siege to the Sydney Journalists' Club. We were put up to it by Germaine Greer, who had come back to promote her book, *The Female Eunuch*. Full of ourselves, after a pep talk from Greer, about fifty of us formed the Media Women's Action Group and within the fortnight we had marched on the club, a tatty old establishment in a lane behind Central Railway.

The club was run by the union all reporters were compelled to join, but the men were to argue for months about admitting women as members. Old hacks who all but lived in the club would meet to remind each other that they had to have some refuge where they could swear without being embarrassed about it, but the four of us on the appropriate committee were busy devising strategies to smoke them out. What I liked most about the cause was making the old codgers as miserable as possible, and little made them more miserable than being elbowed aside in their sanctum sanctorum. Though they drew out the battle for a bit, claiming that the club didn't have enough women's toilets, it was their last stand.

Contemplating victories like that gave us an exaggerated sense of our power. All of a sudden, we seemed to be insiders. Women were upending elements of the established order. Men as free of ambition as the Balmain layabouts knew people who knew people about to determine government policy. Balmain itself was in the news. Reporters wrote about the place as if the dust from the Balmain collieries had no sooner settled than we found ourselves in the middle of Bloomsbury, figuring out whose turn it was to play Virginia Woolf.

Moorhouse, our suburb's unofficial spokesman, had moved in with Sandra Levy, and Don and I went out with them several nights a week. These evenings involved extravagant routines which sounded better on paper than they were in practice. Both men were sybarites who felt as if they were missing out on life's essentials if they went for more than two or three days without eating in an expensive restaurant and swilling its finest wines.

THE OFFICE RADICAL

Moorhouse liked to ritualize everything, including evenings out, and on Saturday nights after dinner he insisted on going to the Journalists' Club, to hear jazz pianist Dick Hughes. At the bar, late one night, I ran into an old police reporter who had voted against admitting women. Smiling manfully, he made a crack about the privileges of membership. 'Not me, mate,' I said. 'I wouldn't join this crummy club.' I nodded at Don and Frank. 'They signed me in . . .'

TWELVE
Among the Literati

My side of the family met Don's father once, and once was more than enough. The old man came to lunch at Headlong Hall, put away half a bottle of Scotch and went upstairs. He reappeared without warning, tumbled all the way down and lay in a little heap at the foot of the stairs, unconscious but otherwise unhurt.

'Drunk's luck,' Don said sourly, after we had wrapped his dad in a blanket and put him on the sofa. He half-woke up, mumbled something about his club and lapsed into unconsciousness again, though the doorbell rang insistently enough to rouse the dead. My parents, who had never before called on me unexpectedly, were outside, with a couple from Holland they were showing around the colourful slums on the wrong side of the city.

'Are we in time for coffee?' my father said expansively, as they trooped in behind him. Don greeted them and vanished into the kitchen, allegedly to put the kettle on. At a loss, I gestured towards the bundle in the blanket. The nice-looking, sturdy, Dutch hausfrau seemed to be hypnotized by the sight. I wondered what it would be like to belong to a family trained to overlook anything that got in the way of the usual conventions. Like a body on the sofa. 'I believe you haven't met Don's father,' I said, in a bright, sociable tone of voice.

'Pleased to meet you . . .'

'He's asleep, dad.' I could have sworn that Don's father had just mumbled, 'You can drop me at the club'.

'You have an interesting house,' said the Dutchman. The curtains at the front were drawn and, as usual, the place was dark as a dungeon.

'What about some coffee?'

'Thank you,' mum edged the others towards the hall, 'we only wanted to say hello . . .'

My mother was always a little formal, in front of Don. 'He seems very nice,' she said carefully, the first time they met, at a dinner at the old house in Harbord. The men had gone outside, as if dad were obeying an atavistic impulse to show off the property — a concrete patch being hemmed in by home units — while we were washing up. I knew that Don's courtly reserve had disconcerted mum, but she wouldn't have dreamed of mentioning it to me. '. . . and very polite,' she said. I laughed.

During dinner, he had looked up in amazement to see that my mother, father and I were into the main course, because he was only half-way through his soup. He had not had a chance to finish his sentences either, since he was thoughtful enough to remain silent as he pondered le mot juste, and all of us opened our mouths to say whatever came into our heads.

'I know what you mean,' mum had said to help him out: in answering a casual question about his thesis he found himself trying to explain something about Norman Mailer's first person narrative, an effort akin to explaining Heisenberg's Uncertainty Principle to people intent on learning English as a second language. 'I know just what you mean,' said mum, 'he makes it all up. That's the trouble with these modern writers, they don't write about real life.' From week to week, she carted home armfuls of historical romances from the Manly Public Library. Teased about reading a potboiler with everyone in fancy dress, she would have asserted equally vigorously that life was tragic enough without having your nose rubbed in it.

I let it pass. I was hoping against hope that she wouldn't launch into an attack on *Portnoy's Complaint*, a novel which outraged her. The sex scenes were bad enough. What kind of Jewish boy would stick his thingummyjig in uncooked liver? Someone who could sneer at his mother like that, that's who. If she started airing her grievances against Philip Roth, before you knew it we would be having an argument which ended with dad accusing me of being an anti-Semite. That was how it usually went, but we were on our best behaviour, more or less, and the conversation drifted until mum, still seeming to feel a need to establish her own literary credentials, mentioned a writer called Vondel.

'Who the fuck is that?' I reined in. It was Don's first visit, after all.

'Pardon?' he said faintly.

'What? You've never heard of Vondel, the Dutch Shakespeare?' Her tone of voice hinted that it was an unimaginable gap in his education, and he looked as if he were having trouble keeping a straight face. I had warned him about Portnoy, but who could have guessed that she would pluck the Dutch Shakespeare out of thin air.

'Of course he hasn't,' I snapped. 'They don't teach books in translation in his department. Not even Proust or Dostoyevsky.'

'Vondel,' said dad.

'Fondle?' Don was obliging to the last.

'Vondel . . .'

'Well, I've never heard of him. I mean it's not as if you taught us a thing about Dutch culture . . .'

'Don't speak to mum like that,' my father said automatically, '. . . would you like some more wine, Don?'

In the kitchen, over the washing up, my mother went on being circumspect until I tried to pick a fight with her and she let me have it, saying that the only puzzle was that any man could put up with me for long. That being my own private opinion, I gave up trying to find out whether or not she approved of Don.

Like any couple, we were oddly matched. He was long-suffering and I was short-tempered. He was dispassionate and I was full of sound and fury. He was gloomily self-contained, and I was regularly in overdrive, unable to dispel the sensation of being on the edge of control. Unless we were in the middle of a row, however, he made me feel less frenzied and distracted.

Not at all traditional about any woman's role, least of all mine, he was buoyed up by my jauntiness, amused by my prickliness and impressed by my refusal to knuckle under. Social occasions could make him edgy, but that wasn't the only reason we sparred in public, trading insults like a couple of vaudevillians hitting each other with a rubber chicken. It was expected of us. People assumed that the relationship was stormier than it was: knowing otherwise gave us a sense of being co-conspirators, almost as if we were allied against the world.

From the way that my family spoke of him, you might have thought he was perfect in every way but one, but we'd been together about eighteen months before the question of his antecedents was raised insistently enough for my mother, of all people, to object to it. Pleased with herself, she couldn't resist telling us about it when we next went to see them.

'You know we were out with the aunts and uncles at the Hakoah Club last week? It's fantastic for the money, that smorgasbord they have — four dollars and we were still so full at night we only had a sandwich . . .'

'Who wants another whisky?'

'Why don't you wait, Paul,' she said quickly, before Don could reply. 'We're eating in a few minutes.'

'What was that about the Hakoah Club?' Deconstructionist or not, Don liked his stories nicely rounded off.

'That smorgasbord is first-class,' said my father, 'really first-class.'

'The aunts and uncles were all saying how much they liked Don, and then Nick said, "what a pity he isn't Jewish". "Yes, it really is a shame," Nan said, "when he's such a nice man . . ." You know how they go on. I was sick of hearing it already, and

I told them,' mum looked around triumphantly, 'if it's so important to you, why don't you pay him to convert?' Don laughed the hardest of all. 'I knew you would like it,' she said at last, pink-faced with success, 'and that's exactly what I told them. I said, "make him an offer. You never know . . ." '

I marvelled at her getting away with it, parodying the others for attitudes she disowned and still managed to air. If I'd heard 'pity he isn't Jewish' once, I'd heard it a dozen times, and it still made me bristle. Buried in there somewhere was the implication that I had turned my back on my own.

It was made explicit, curiously enough, only if we argued about Israel, when the mildest remark about Palestinian rights drove my father into a frenzy. You might have thought that I had volunteered to be Yasser Arafat's publicist in Sydney. If the argument went further, dad was sure to mention the war, saying that my relatives had been murdered by the Nazis, and here I was, siding with the enemies of the Jews.

This grotesque accusation would have startled anyone but a Jew. It was the old equation, based on the logic of guilt, and it had been drummed into my generation from the start. If it made no sense, nor did my response. The sense of guilt surfaced, deviously, at especially awkward moments. I failed to analyze the impulse behind it, but I would find myself blurting out that I was Jewish in a situation in which this absurd revelation would cause equally absurd embarrassment all round.

'. . . well, I'm Jewish,' I said, briefly managing to silence all the people at the table, on the one and only occasion I was invited to dinner by the head of Don's department at the university. Wilkes, the lanky professor who had been busy waging war on the Leavisites when I was a fresher, was so taciturn that he seemed to be holding himself aloof from anything that could ruffle the smooth and even flow of his important thoughts. If someone intruded on him, he retreated into irony. In the corridors of the English department, he might incline his head a quarter-inch or so, by way of a greeting, and then again, he might not.

'I bet he said, "and bring whatsername",' I grumbled when Don told me about the invitation, but I was resolved to be restraint itself. The function, a farewell to someone going on sabbatical leave, was held in a small dining room of the university staff club. Having fixed on my name, Wilkes was obviously determined to use it. 'Would Elisabeth like some sherry?' he asked, almost as soon as we arrived.

'Oh yes, please,' I said ardently, tossing it down at a gulp in order not to taste it.

The guests, seemingly picked at random from what Mrs Wilkes, a severe, stockily-built woman with blue-grey hair, probably called 'the younger set', included a lecturer who had just arrived from England and looked unhappy about it, the lecturer who was going to England on sabbatical and kept saying he would as soon stay home, and writer David Malouf, then a tutor in the department. On any normal occasion, Malouf could be relied on to be the best company in the world. This occasion was different. It was hard to fight off the impression that one had strayed into an Evelyn Waugh parody of academic life.

'Shall we, Gerald?' said Mrs W., who was at one end of the table, rising briskly to her feet when we were about halfway through the meal. Wilkes obediently unfurled himself and they set off, going in opposite directions on either side of the table, like a pair of young lovers about to play chasing; but no, all they did was swap places.

'Do they do that at proper dinners in Cambridge?' I whispered to the man next to me, the new lecturer, who although sallow and emaciated-looking had cheered up tremendously at the sight of the greyish beef and roast potatoes. It wasn't the first time I had noticed people from Britain attacking food as if they had a race memory of rationing. 'Swap chairs, I mean.'

'I very much doubt it,' he whispered back. 'What was it you were saying about the icecream cake?'

But even the Bombe Alaska, rumoured to be the professor's

one weakness, failed to liven up an atmosphere so muted that
there were pauses during which you heard nothing but the
clinking of glasses and the clearing of throats. The woman
opposite, whose frumpishness hinted that she liked to think of
herself as a bluestocking, was saying that not enough children
were taught the classics. But she spoke without passion, as if it
were over-rehearsed and, perhaps maliciously, I asked if she
taught. It sounded so direct that I wondered if Mrs Wilkes
would tap her glass, like Lady Astor, and call for general conversation. 'Oh, I'm just someone's wife,' she said, with a tiny, affected laugh.

The evening dragged on like that, with one achingly civilized
moment after another. I seem to get carried away when people
are being polite, as if I am determined to prove that I am at least
as loud and outlandish as they suspected all along. Though I no
longer have the slightest idea why, I suddenly blurted out that I
was Jewish and as if that were not ridiculous enough, I sounded
as if I were throwing down the gauntlet.

No-one said, '. . . you don't look Jewish'. In fact they didn't
say anything at all, and I imagined I heard my voice echoing,
much as one hears oneself, waking at four in the morning after
too much whisky and too much coffee, when the replay
resounds like a lapse people will remember for life.

The conversation had picked up again. Don, who was seated
next to the bluestocking, had a faraway look in his eyes, as if he
were checking his memory against the first hundred stanzas of
the *Cantos*. I knew exactly what that meant. He was accustomed to my lack of tact, but this particular outburst had taken
him by surprise. He would console me later on, but for the
moment he was wondering what had happened to the waiter,
and if he had a faraway look in his eyes, he was about to get
paralytic.

Outwardly the most imperturbable of men, he coped with the
strains of social life by absenting himself as best he could. People
who didn't know him well said he was standoffish or interpreted

his silence as condescension. He could be ferociously funny, but he was uninterested in gossip and slow to engage in small talk, instead listening as if his mind were elsewhere. Since he was relaxed enough around me to let some of his defences down, I rattled on at him regardless, very possibly the reason I was slow to recognize our first fully-fledged domestic crisis.

In the spring I came back from a vacation abroad, airily confessed to the usual indiscretions and took two days to notice that he looked a bit washed-out. Not only was he seeing another woman, he couldn't decide between us. Shouting at him didn't seem to clear things up, so I stepped out of character and kept quiet about it. In fact, I was so nauseatingly civilized I could have passed for a Protestant. Perhaps I should admit that this role was scripted for me by my rival, a graduate student who was at Don day and night to move out of Headlong Hall.

Occasionally we ran into each other at the Forest Lodge Hotel and smiled through gritted teeth, a performance which became less plausible after she sent the first of a series of telegrams threatening to kill herself. One telegram turned up while he was in the middle of a tutorial on *Moby Dick*. I could have told her that it was not the way to win his heart.

Despite his admiration for a level of intensity to which he did not aspire, despite his liking for scenes that smacked of a literary imagination (as long as he were uninvolved), he discouraged public displays of emotion. The previous summer I had fallen off a ferry in the middle of the harbour. It was no big deal. Someone had rented a ferry that evening for a party, and I went into the drink because I was showing off by dancing on the rim of the deck, outside the safety rail. No-one seemed to notice and I was too mortified to call out. I concentrated on getting off my new, tight jeans so I could swim to Shark Island, perhaps a quarter-of-a-mile away, though it was hard to tell in the dark. The moment my jeans were off, I had to struggle to get them on again, because the ferry was turning and so many people had rushed over to one side that the captain was shouting over the public address system that the boat would capsize if they didn't move.

I wished they would just go away. Never in my life had I been so embarrassed, and of course, it was even worse having to be hauled in over the side like the one that didn't get away, barely able to wriggle because my jeans had shrunk about three sizes. 'I saved you,' someone whispered seductively, 'do you want a dance?'

Don was nowhere in sight. Later I heard that he had behaved with perfect decorum. He was with a couple of friends when someone rushed up gibbering that I had fallen in the water. 'You win some, you lose some,' said Don, and had another drink.

Clearly he was not the man to lure away with a promise of suicide and sensing some slight advantage, I asked him about his plans one Sunday morning in October, when we were having brunch at the pancake place in Kings Cross, where American innocents on leave from Vietnam went for a taste of home cooking. He said he planned to have the lemon pancakes, and asked if I wanted to get married, adding a little sheepishly that it would make my parents happy.

In fact, my mother was horrified. We had decided that the only stylish way out of it was to marry on the second of December, the date of the federal election, and it gave her less than five weeks to prepare for the big day. The very thought of introducing some of the people from the Forth and Clyde to my family was enough to make anyone break out in a cold sweat.

The moment she heard that we were to be married, my friend Liz Fell had asked if I were pregnant, glared at me disbelievingly and cornered me for a pep talk on abortion. But the family wasn't to be trusted either. If we asked the Englishman, mum was sure to sidle up, maliciously, and ask about his writing. 'It's all right,' I assured her, preparing to edit her guest list as well, 'we don't want to overdo it . . .'

As a matter of fact, the few people invited to the wedding ceremony at the registry office outdid themselves. Frank Moorhouse and Stephen Knight pranced about in straw boaters, gear which struck just the right note of levity or added to the ritual, depending on your preference. Sandra Levy wore a teeshirt dress without a brassiere, giving my uncles something to think about while we waited outside for our turn. It was hardly worth the wait. The clerk officiating at the ceremony, an apologetic little man in a mustard-coloured suit, mumbled so inaudibly that almost all we heard, from beginning to end, was Uncle Nick's running commentary on his performance.

'That was quick,' he boomed, unabashed, as we posed for photographs on the registry office steps, dodging the rice thrown at another happy couple, 'and what a nebbish. I couldn't hear a word he said.' Nick had spoken in Dutch and Sandra Levy asked for a translation. 'We hear that you're in television now, Sandra,' said Aunty Nan, scowling at her husband, 'that must be very interesting.'

The lunch was at my parents' place. They had sold the cottage in Harbord and bought a house in Balgowlah Heights, high up on a steep, terraced block of land which overlooked Middle Harbour. It was impossible to visit the house without oohing and ahing over the view. Guests would be led to the windows or out to the balcony at the front and cued-in. 'I always say it's the best view in the world . . .' Putting down the champagne bottle unopened, a gesture that made Don, for one, glance at him in alarm, my father raised his hand with a flourish, as if to unveil the bays and inlets of the drab green foreshores, before turning his attention to the Spit Bridge.

'It's true. You do always say that . . .'

'Would you like some help with that bottle, Paul?'

'We shouldn't ask you to work at your own wedding.' He was still fumbling with the napkin around the bottle's neck, as if it mattered.

'Hurry up, dad, we're dying of thirst.'

'It's a terrific poster.' Sandra could be relied on to be tactful. My mother had commissioned *Don's Party* posters from the guy who did the sale signs for her dress shop. The original *Don's*

Party, a play by David Williamson, had been set on the night of the previous federal election. 'Well, we're nearly all Whitlam supporters here,' said mum, her arch tone a signal of some sort.

But if there were an agreement about protocol, Uncle Bram chose to ignore it, muttering that he was still capable of speaking for himself, even if they disagreed. In Sydney, back in the nineteen-fifties, the family had shed the old left-of-centre political affiliations like so much reffo baggage done up with string. Uncle Bram, who owned four taxis and called himself a company director, was only a fraction less conservative than Uncle Nick. My mother liked to think of herself as a progressive, which forced her to find original excuses for voting for the Liberals. This time around she had trumpeted her intention of deserting them and dad had followed suit. Voting for Labor once, bright and early that morning, gave him the sort of opening he liked, and he accused his brother-in-law of being inflexible.

'You don't even know who I voted for,' Uncle Bram said crossly.

'The best man, I hope.'

'That's my son-in-law,' dad said to no-one in particular and I imagined him trying to introduce Don to the crowd at the bar of the Pacific Hotel in Manly. 'Got the certificate to prove it.'

'I think they know who he is, dad.'

'Don't stand on ceremony, please don't stand on ceremony,' carolled my mother, sounding as if she were trying out for a Noel Coward production in some small town in Indonesia. Five minutes more of this and she would speak in an English accent.

'So eat already,' Don said.

Without a doubt, the family had prepared itself to meet the intellectuals, and over lunch the uncles were positively frisky. Never before had they been so close to a dirty writer, and in what may have been intended as a homage to Moorhouse, they told off-colour jokes and then apologized to 'the girls', who looked uneasy and tried to laugh.

'I wish they'd save their jokes for the bowling club.'

'Is anyone here shocked?' said mum, but she refrained from remarking on the sophistication of my friends. I had made her promise not to tackle Moorhouse about the depraved literature in *Tabloid Story*. She had picked up a copy at Headlong Hall, and without so much as glancing at it, had shown it to some visitors who asked what my talented friends were up to these days.

Aunty Ali, who had heard several versions of this story, rapidly turned to Frank and started talking about her book club. Of course the conversation wound up in the wrong place, with one or other of the aunts asking him what he really thought of *Portnoy's Complaint*. Instead of answering right away, Moorhouse stared so lasciviously at the salmon mousse that I wondered it he were about to strip and stick his dick in it, to demystify the sacrilege. It would have been more in his line to say that Philip Roth did not go far enough, but he didn't do that either, and mustering his very considerable charm to focus it like a spotlight over the table on Aunty Nan, who blushed, he asked her what she thought of censorship.

'Listen to him, it sounds as if he's getting ready for the Country Women's Association.'

'I couldn't say I was an expert,' said Nan, stuck for an answer for the first time in years.

'Would you like more champagne, Don?'

'Ask him if he wants a beer to take away the feeling of fullness.' My mother was rehearsing for 'Private Lives' again. 'I never cry at weddings,' she told Stephen Knight, who said that he tried to adhere to the same policy.

'Your family's amazing. Are they always like this?' Stephen's friend, who was from New Zealand, may never have heard so many people talking at once. She looked exhausted and no wonder, with the uncles vying for her attention.

'Usually they're noisier,' Don whispered.

'Don said they're usually noisier.'

'No, I didn't mean that . . .' Poor Janet. Uncle Nick was giving her a step-by-step account of a holiday in New Zealand, and he hadn't even got to the first fiord.

'. . . even pornography,' Moorhouse intoned, solemn as a judge.

Sandra was still arguing with Cousin Ron, a lawyer who had grown to be at least as stiff-necked as his father. Though he may well have been teasing, he had just asserted that the Australian Broadcasting Commission was run by a bunch of left-wingers. 'Like that velveteened Marxist toad, Duckmanton,' said Don, suddenly joining in.

I smiled at him across the table. 'Did I ever tell you his daughter was at Frensham?'

'The mistress of the non sequitur . . .'

'Don't fucking get snaky with me now we're married. If you're Jewish, you only have to say "I divorce you, I divorce you, I divorce you," and that's it.'

'A toast to the bride and groom,' said my father, all unawares.

'Wait a moment, Paul . . .'

'What about the cake?' That was Uncle Nick, of course.

'I've got a message from Jules.' I picked up the telegram my brother had sent from Jerusalem. Out of the corner of my eye, I could see my father fumbling in his pockets for the telegrams he was supposed to have hidden. 'He says vote early and vote often.'

'You're making it up.' My cousin looked really disgusted.

'Shows how much you know, Blue. Don made it up.'

'A toast to the bride and groom . . .'

'Not yet,' said my mother firmly.

Away from Home

Nancy Reagan and I met in a hotel room in Chicago, where she had posed on a flowered chintz sofa, as if expecting a photographer instead of a mere reporter. She sat with one arm trailing along the top of the sofa, one ankle tucked behind the other and her high-heeled shoes off, a hint of girlish informality which made her performance all the more disconcerting. In answer to almost any question she murmured 'yes' or 'no', or more likely stared thoughtfully into space, opening her eyes a little wider as she adjusted the mask of her face into what may have been an expression of distant anticipation. The first time it happened, I repeated myself loudly, wondering if the woman was deaf. Instead of answering, she inclined her head a fraction of an inch. I rephrased the question and she drummed her fingers on the sofa, a trifle impatiently.

I had interviewed the wives of other American politicians. Scared witless of saying the wrong thing, they restricted themselves to remarks like, 'people know he is a team player . . .' or '. . . no, I wouldn't say he's a politician, he's a statesman'. But Mrs Reagan left her rivals for dead. After asking her twenty questions, I had scribbled a couple of sentences into my notebook, and one was, 'Oh no, he's a statesman . . .'

It wouldn't have mattered what she said, as long as she said enough to pad out the 'exclusive interview' I had promised the editor. Intent on getting her to talk, I failed to ask a single sticky question, but it was all to no avail. The minutes dragged on.

'Have you been to Australia?' Talk about being obvious. 'Yes,' said Mrs Reagan. Under my breath, I slowly counted to ten. 'Did you like it?' I said through gritted teeth. 'Yes,' she murmured, and again lapsed into silence. Was this what I came to America for?

I left Sydney in 1978. Don and I were separating. We were too friendly to have split up and stayed in the same city, and we continued to reassure each other for about two years that we were separated only by distance, telling anyone who asked that I was in New York for the sake of my career. I had made my reputation as a journalist with a series of profiles for the *National Times*. The profiles had a sly innocence which undermined the pretensions of public figures, and people gossiped about them knowingly. I liked the recognition, but after a couple of years with the newspaper it made me feel claustrophobic, as if I might be hearing the same words from the same mouths until the day I died. The world in which I lived suddenly seemed confined: in moments of despair, I imagined that my only identity was as a *National Times* feature writer, whose life consisted of a series of empty performances.

I wanted to slow down and take stock, and it wasn't possible in Sydney, where I felt trapped in a role of my own making. I was boyish, boisterous and theatrical. I courted attention and wore costume, going to parties in a sailor suit, and to work in a second-hand pair of overalls from a Rolls Royce factory in England.

I stopped wearing costumes in New York. I liked being anonymous. No-one cared what I thought, no-one noticed what I did, no-one expected a thing from me. It was as if I were free to reinvent myself, an illusion with a logic all its own in America, where a distortion of history gave rise to the pervasive myth that it was possible to throw off the shackles and begin again. Instead of dreaming up another self, I stubbed my toe against intractable reality and came up against the same old limitations, but I managed to cling to the liberating notion that my life was my own invention.

I was dazzled by New York. Against all expectation, I fell in love with the city the first time I caught the subway. I emerged in the financial district, marvelled over the graceful skyscrapers of Wall Street, and wheeled around to see the spire of Trinity Church and, in the churchyard, tombstones weathered into ghostly shapes. Dawdling down Wall Street, I washed up at the river's edge, barely noticing the filth and flotsam though I stood for half an hour listening to the mysterious hum from the reverberations of the cables on the Brooklyn Bridge. Other people said that they were energized by New York's frenzied pace, but I was dreamily entranced, like a tourist with all the time in the world.

I saw the city as other than it was, filtering out the public squalor of the present to conjure up a make-believe past, set in the old ghetto on the Lower East Side. The children and grandchildren of the original immigrants had long since fled to the suburbs of Westchester and Long Island, and only a handful of poor, elderly Jews were left. I identified with them, straining at a sense of shared experience I had resisted in Sydney, where acknowledging it risked capitulating to the claims of family and community. In Sydney, I had sealed myself off from my family's past; in New York, I dreamed up connections out of a longing for the past. I left behind my family, and imagined myself surrounded by family. Ten thousand miles from home, I felt at home.

After about a year in New York, I went to shul on Yom Kippur, out of curiosity. People strolled into the synagogue in Greenwich Village in blue jeans, and one man was in a pair of shorts, attire which would have created a fuss, back in the Temple Emanuel in Woollahra. Instead of pretending to fast (let alone fasting), some of the locals hung around outside, wolfing down slices of pizza before they went in. I didn't stay long, but I made another subliminal gesture towards atonement five years later, going to the Gay Synagogue, where lesbians in prayer shawls played a role usually reserved for men, at least in my experience, by reading out parts of the service. This aside, it wasn't much different from going to shul with heterosexuals or venturing into the Abyssinian Baptist Church in Harlem for a Sunday morning service, because I was an intruder, checking out the customs of the natives. I said that I felt at home in New York. I guess I should have said that you don't have to be Jewish to be a rootless cosmopolitan, but it helps: even now, after eleven years in the New Jerusalem, I need to know that I can pick up and leave, any time at all . . .

I live in a loft on the first floor of a converted warehouse, downtown in Manhattan. The average New Yorker has an apartment which could pass for a walk-in closet. Not me: I can get my exercise walking from one end of the loft to the other. In here, small islands of second-hand furniture are surrounded by acres of empty space. Like everything else, it has its drawbacks, of course. This is the textile district: during the working week, truck drivers double-park outside, engines idling, to argue at the tops of their voices with the guys who are supposed to unload the bolts of cloth. What with them and the trucks, the buses, the sirens and the cacophony of horns as one car after another swerves into the middle lane, life in my loft is about as restful as camping out on a construction site.

Chinatown is three blocks east, on the other side of the Tombs, a high-rise prison. TriBeCa, west of Broadway, has been gentrified, and is so fashionable that stretch limousines pull up outside bars with trademark cocktails in unnatural colours. This block is steadfastly unfashionable, however. The *New York Times* hasn't sent anyone to do a feature on the local diner. Flocks of tourists do not pour out of buses to stand gawping at the gems of cast-iron construction. The town planners haven't given us a name, and I've come to think of my bit of Broadway as the Lower Depths.

We do have a claim to fame, however, because the alley at the back of the building is always being filmed. Dark, dank and dangerous-looking, it's regarded as the city's most photogenic alley; only the other week, a stuntman did backwards somersaults off our fire escape, after a crime show shootout. In fact, the people in this building are talking about putting in for residuals.

My neighbours are painters, sculptors and artistes. Some of the top floor is rented out to performance artists who howl while they dance. The guy on the second floor makes sculptures so large that they have to be disassembled the moment he completes them. The silent Japanese in the loft behind my place is a pointillist painter who covers wall-sized canvases with white or yellow dots all but invisible to the naked eye. It can be difficult to distinguish between the precocious and the mature work, but what he used to do was cover a wall-sized canvas with white or yellow paint put on with a roller. Just before his pictures go on show, they're dragged out, past my dining room table. Did I mention that I live in New York's largest unofficial passageway? In working hours, when the freight elevator at the back is being used, the only way for the painter and his wife to get in and out is through my place. If they have visitors, detachments of Japanese shuffle through, bowing to no-one in particular.

It's like living in Grand Central Station. Ten minutes ago, the painter's skittish wife came clattering over the parquet floor. 'It's Saturday,' I said loudly. On Saturdays, the neighbours are supposed to go out the back way, but she glared and said, '... elevator broken'. This, the first phrase in English she acquired, is a euphemism for 'put a sock in it, round-eyes, I'm going through'. I glared at her, too. In addition to the usual outlandish clothes, she had a fur cone on her head. Every time I see her I get culture shock. Still, I should be grateful.

Shortly after I moved in here six years ago, the painter went off to Tokyo for the summer, but he had sublet his half of the floor to no fewer than six of his compatriots and, as if that wasn't confusing enough, there was a knock on the door one morning and when I opened it I found two plainclothes policemen, one of whom flashed a badge, and said, by way of preamble: 'We've come about the body in the alley . . .' He wasn't kidding, as I heard when I put a glass against the wall to listen to the cops talking to someone out the back. One of the Japanese had contracted a mysterious 48-hour virus, the original 48-hour virus, because he died, just like that, as he was being lifted into an ambulance parked in the alley. I couldn't believe that they'd gone to the trouble of using the freight elevator, for once.

The telephone rang, and as the lodger dived to answer it, the jackhammers started up again. It's always happening just as things seem to have quietened down outside and by now our bit of Broadway looks to have been strip-mined. Con Edison burrows around for gas leaks. The deconstruction crews from public works trace corroded water lines. New York Telephone makes its underground connections. The Department of Highways fiddles with the cracked, crumbling footpath, but only because it is about to cave in on the subway platform. Here in the Lower Depths, if you feel the ground sliding from under you, it probably is.

The lodger mouthed something, but I had guessed what it was. Telephone therapy time. Chapter 61. My friend Reggie is in love with A Married Man. 'It's finished,' she snuffled, mumbling about throwing something off the balcony, before she burst into tears. Reggie spends half her waking life attending to the ebb and flow of her emotions but it is unlike her to be quite so melodramatic. 'Stay where you are,' I said, sounding as if I'd pinched some soap-opera script, 'I'll be right over.' But she was suicidal because her two-day-old video cassette recorder was on the fritz. I assumed it was a blown fuse; she thought of it as the final act of an original tragedy. Americans are raised to expect that things will get better. It is scant preparation for life.

'Will you call Crazy Eddy's?' she whispered brokenly.

Crazy Eddy's was once just an electronics store in the way that Bedlam was once just a neighbourhood clinic. Le tout New York goes to Crazy Eddy's on Saturday. One time I did too, and watched three sweating salesmen dematerialize before my eyes because all I wanted was a lousy $229 ghetto blaster. Doubtless you have to bribe them to accept a pittance like that.

So there I was with my delicate mission, calling Crazy Eddy's. A real New Yorker knows that the only way to make the stranger at the other end of the telephone shut up and listen is by starting off the conversation with a barrage of abuse, but as the switchgirl at Crazy Eddy's had doubtless been insulted all morning, I tried another tack, whispering that I didn't know who to ask for. 'What?' she roared, but it worked — instead of ordering me to call the repair department on Monday, she put me through.

The repairmen are conditioned to say something along the lines of, 'Haul ass, sister, and bring your broken appliance in here . . .' That's what they told me when my $229 boom-box went on the blink about a minute and a half after the warranty expired. On that occasion, I swathed the radio in plastic, and walked over to the store in the Village, whistling the theme from 'Elvira Madigan' because I was worried about being taken for a disco-lover. 'It's easier if you carry it around by the handle,' the repairman had said, nonchalantly. He didn't mend it, though. 'Thassright, lady, we sell 'em, but we don't fix 'em. Send it to Hitachi, they got a factory in New Jersey . . . Waddya mean "how?" Way you had this thing wrapped, you just need a stamp, mail it right out . . .'

I was employed a month or two after I arrived in New York, but the nature of the work left something to be desired: I'd been taken on as a correspondent for the *Australian Women's Weekly*. The company's office in New York was run by a small, red-faced man called McGann, whose icons included a sweat-stained Akubra which had belonged to his late employer, Sir Frank Packer. McGann and I disliked each other on sight, and in his case the emotion turned to violent loathing after he wandered in from lunch one day to find me prancing around in Packer's hat. As a rule, we argued instead about my coming in late.

In other respects the routine was less than taxing. If an editor cabled from Sydney, one of the three reporters in the office ambled off to investigate face-lifts by acupuncture or the last word in post-modern diet therapy, a regime from which I escaped by dreaming up an assignment which allowed me to travel around the country for the best part of a year. I talked Ita Buttrose, the boss of the *Weekly*, into letting me cover the 1980 presidential election. I assure you that it was a coup. I was on the campaign trail for a magazine which didn't cover American politics, and when there was some murmuring about it from Sydney, I dressed up the assignment, by interviewing the candidates' wives.

They didn't have anything to gain from talking to me, but one of my assets as a reporter is that I can be persuasive — okay, manipulative — over the 'phone. It doesn't work as well in person — press flacks and political hopefuls sense something insurrectionary in my presence if I forget to make nice for a moment. In 1980, fierce Barbara Bush sensed it so quickly that she tried to wriggle out of the interview, discovered that it was all locked up, and sat there glowering at me across the back seat of a campaign car, knitting like Madam Defarge. Plain, purl, off with her head. At least she departed from the script. The others spoke as if they were on automatic replay and I kept wondering if it mattered to my readers. Much as I may have fancied myself a sharp-eyed, sceptical observer of the scene, I was writing about it for a magazine full of knitting patterns and pictures of royal babies.

Of course there were compensations. It delighted me to make

the job fit my requirements, regardless of the requirements of my employer. I saw a great deal of the country, I surveyed the drawn-out political charade from the perspective of the people at the back of the crowd — my natural habitat as a reporter — and I managed to arrange my schedule around the demands of my private life.

I was involved with another reporter on the campaign trail, an Englishman who lived in Washington with his wife and family. Neither of us let them get in our way, and at first we were ridiculously happy. Was that why I was in America? Damn right. I'd known nothing like it. I didn't trust my impulses and I didn't trust his. But it was an idyll — the full catastrophe — half-empty glasses, deliquescent moments, delirium, in a series of strange rooms, hotel rooms for which one of us would claim expenses. His newspaper picked up the tab for the Ritz Carlton in Chicago, where the breakfast trolley was laid with silver plate. I had moved out of the Holiday Inn (where breakfast was a Danish in cellophane and coffee in styrofoam), but Australian Consolidated Press picked up the tab for the Dom Perignon. Later I wondered whether the expenses form was the objective correlative of our romance: someone else was paying, for the moment. I didn't know the romance was doomed, though. Nor did he, it seems, because he left his family and moved in with me. 'You have a very bad temper,' he said, pressed for his version of events after he moved out. That was it, his A to Z analysis of two years of domestic turmoil.

I was on the loose again. Reluctant to join the swelling chorus of single women who admitted to looking for love, I said I was interested in lust. Of course I still spent about half my life on the 'phone with my girlfriends, moaning about the shortage of single men. I remember one conversation in particular. I was on the way back from Sydney, and having landed in Los Angeles with five hours to kill before the flight to New York, I fled the airport and called my friend Reggie from a pay phone on Santa Monica pier. It was a grey winter day. The only other people on the pier were three long-haired drifters, one of whom had just accused me of being indifferent to the plight of the Vietnam vets. 'I hate it here,' I wailed into the phone.

'It's worse than you think,' Reggie said cheerfully. 'There's new figures out. Women our age have more chance of being kidnapped by terrorists than getting married . . .'

Instead of waiting around for Mr Right, I opted for out-of-town tryouts, if I was on the road, picking up for a few days with a married man. But the register of men I wouldn't have dreamed of introducing to my friends included a widower who sold vacuum cleaners, a retired colonel from the Canadian army who kept talking about Clausewitz, a clean-cut boy from Colgate University who couldn't get over the fact that I had a Lou Reed record, *at my age*, and a millionaire with dyed hair I met in New York at a wedding.

In his case, I was hesitant enough to let him court me for a fortnight. I don't like rich men and I should have known better than to go home with the guy with the Grecian Formula hair. He owned a building a couple of blocks from Wall Street. We stepped out of the elevator into his living room and I stared around me, aghast. The place was crammed from floor to ceiling with Judaica. 'This is worse than the Jewish Museum,' I said, 'it'd be like fucking in a shul . . .' The question was moot. He didn't get it up, and he had the effrontery to claim that it was because I kept talking about my mother. He was imagining it. All I had said, after seeing his bedroom, was: 'My mother should see me now.' On the wall, above the bed, was a framed front page from the *New York Times*, with a monumental headline about the Yom Kippur War.

By that time, I was a correspondent for the *National Times*, a position I relished, although the editor and I seldom agreed about my interpretation of my role. The newspaper was then in its most obsessive muck-racking phase. I was expected to track down the gangsters and CIA operatives who may or may not have known something about what had gone on behind the scenes in Australia. Failing that, I was meant to be in Washington D.C., sifting through documents which had just been declassified. Instead I would be stuck in a farm kitchen in the backblocks of Iowa — interviewing a middle-American housewife who, to my horror, had turned out to be a raving Jesus freak — or in Macy's department store, interviewing Barbara Cartland, whose face looked as if it might shatter at any moment. It has to be said that I exhibited wayward leanings for a foreign correspondent, and the editor, Brian Toohey, may have said something of the sort before trying to recall me. I told him to get stuffed, and stayed where I was, although the alternative to a senior job in Sydney was no job at all. I was outraged by his proposal, because I was arrogant enough to believe that no-one else had the right to limit my options. Wrong again. He gave me six months to think it over, and then he gave me the sack. I took it hard, and it was a long time before I shrugged off the sense of failure, by turning it into a piece of my past. But instead of fleeing New York, I freelanced, and lived from hand to mouth.

Four years ago, while I was still struggling to make ends meet, Don Anderson telephoned from Sydney before going abroad. He and his wife were to stay in a hotel in New York, and he was wondering if his three-year-old son and the boy's nanny could stay with me. 'I know we have a civilized relationship,' I said, 'but isn't this overdoing it?'

'Is ten days too long?' he murmured, as I concentrated on a different question. 'You're not really travelling with a nanny?' My ex-husband is a man of high style who went into mourning when his shirtmaker in London shuffled off this mortal coil. No-one could have guessed. Don was as perfectly turned-out as ever. I myself couldn't believe it when I'd seen him in Sydney wearing a faintly-frayed shirt, a lapse explained by the sight of his son, who toddled about in tiny, handmade Italian shoes.

This prodigy now proved to have a nanny with connections. 'When someone asked Caroline, the girl who looks after Hugo, if she had friends in New York,' said Don, 'she mentioned some people called Bloomingdale.'

'Like in Bloomingdale's, on 59th and Lexington?'

'That's right,' he said drily. I telephoned a girlfriend the second he had hung up. 'I don't believe it,' I said, 'seven years roughing it in New York, and I'm about to be shown up by my ex-husband's babysitter.'

Okay, I was exaggerating. I have my fits of nostalgie de la boue — indulging what a friend of mine calls my gas-ring mentality — but I live well. I've managed to focus on the essentials, the freedom to travel frequently, and the assurance that I'll earn enough to get by from work I find satisfying. Nowadays I work for the Melbourne *Age*. Though based in New York, I take off for London every so often, and spend two or three months of the summer in Sydney. I go to Sydney to spend time with my family, time that is all the more important now my parents are getting old. I catch up with friends, I keep up a sense of connection, continuing to work for my newspaper, and just as I find myself almost comfortably re-established, I head back to New York, seldom without agonizing about it, seldom without wondering at my detachment.

I've spent more than half my working life in the United States and I'm still on the sidelines. I don't think of myself as an immigrant. I've made lasting friendships but I've failed to strike roots, and when I contemplate going back for good, I tell myself that at least I'd be an insider, writing articles that have some resonance for the people around me. It's tempting, but not tempting enough.

Australia is paradoxical. The country has been transformed without traumatic social upheaval. Sydney not only looks different, but is in danger of losing its identity to the slick internationalism reputed to lure rich tourists. Like many half-hearted exiles, I feel proprietorial about the place I left behind. I find it disconcerting to be fighting for space on the outside deck of a Manly hydrofoil with a bunch of tourists frantically clicking their cameras at *my* harbour. But when I think about the place from this distance it's as if nothing has changed, as if, ten years from now, I'd be arranging to interview people I first interviewed more than ten years ago.

I can foresee it. Life would be easier. I'd live in an apartment looking out to sea. I'd write feature articles for one of the few decent publications in the country, unless Rupert Murdoch has laid claim to them all. Though regretful at first, I'd fit in again, almost as if I'd never left, and that's the trouble. I don't want the continuing uncertainties of my life resolved from one day to the next. It would make me feel I was sinking into middle age.

The other month, I was asked to address a group of women in the media about being a foreign correspondent. I agreed for once and found myself, first thing in the morning, in the conference room of a hotel on Lexington Avenue, face to face with a gaggle of earnest professionals in Nikes and necklaces. The other two women on the panel spoke for ages. I kept it short, fielded a few questions from a blonde who seemed to have modelled herself on Faye Dunaway in *Network*, and was about to slope off when the moderator said she wanted to put in her two-cents worth. Turning to me, she asked where I hoped to be in five years. Nineteen-ninety-something? I couldn't have told her where I expected to be the following week. 'Gee, I don't know,' I said startled, 'I just met this guy . . .'

Acknowledgements

I want to thank my editors Bruce Sims and Clare O'Brien for their patient advice and generous encouragement. With thanks to Inna Cymlich, Patrick Brogan, Reggie Nadelson, Chris Hegedus and D.A. Pennebaker, who saw me through. I am pleased to acknowledge the financial assistance provided by the Literature Board of the Australia Council.

The Penguin Book of Australian Autobiography
A lively and stimulating introduction to more than forty Australians who write of their own lives.
Edited and introduced by John and Dorothy Colmer.

Who am I? What makes me an Australian?

These are two of the questions that the writers in this richly rewarding anthology of Australian autobiography seek to answer. They celebrate the magic world of childhood; the painful struggle towards self-discovery and self-realisation; the impact of two World Wars and the Great Depression; the artist's conflicting loyalties to European and Australian culture and the joys and disappointments of worldly success.

Stirring the Possum

A political autobiography by James McClelland.

From his days as a young Trotskyist in the 1940s—secretly in love with an enemy Stalinist—to his role in the 80s as commissioner in an inquiry into the Maralinga nuclear tests, Jim McClelland has been known as a stirrer.

In his autobiography he offers us a perspective on Australian politics that spans 50 years. His critical assessment of public figures is both humorous and acerbic and includes insight into characters such as Robert Menzies, Lionel Murphy, John Kerr and Neville Wran.

As a trade union lawyer in the early days of workers' compensation, McClelland confronted both idealism and corruption. In the 1950s he had a box seat view of the Labor Party split alongside his old schoolmate Bob Santamaria. He became a Senator in the 1970s and a minister in the Labor government. Then with growing disillusionment he watched his old friend John Kerr dismiss Whitlam from office in 1975. Three years later, he resigned from politics and went back to the law, being appointed Chief Judge of the innovative NSW Land and Environment Court in 1980.

To each of these arenas Jim McCelland brought his energy, his sharp mind and his unfailing capacity to 'liven things up'.

The Puzzles of Childhood Manning Clark

'This book records what lives on in my memory. It is not based on research into the history of either my mother's or my father's family. It makes some use of the material collected for *A History of Australia*. It may help to explain my choice of themes for that history. Who knows? It is my memory of what happened, my memory being my way of moving out of the darkness into the light.'

The Puzzles of Childhood takes us on a journey through the early life of Manning Clark as he follows the confused path to self-understanding, signposted by attempts to understand others.

Whole Life: an autobiography Morris Lurie

'. . . reflects precisely the nature of early childhood memory . . . very much through the eye of the child, a feat which remains truly possible only in the realm of poetry. And Lurie does it superbly.'

Ron Elisha, *Aust. Book Review*

Morris Lurie writes: This is an autobiography, but of a certain kind. Its business is not with nostalgia or sentimentality, with story or anecdote, with the make of hat my father wore, the brand of tea we drank, the particularity of place names, all fine and comforting things, but not the business here. The business here is otherwise. It is to unravel. It is to make plain. It is to investigate why I am how I am. That is the question it addresses, its sole concern. It seeks those harder bones.

'sizzles and crackles with vim and energy'

Anthony Clare, *Age*

'It is a fascinating balance, sometimes near the edge of hysteria, sometimes near comic riot, and beneath it all, for all the apparent lucidity and clarity, something dark and bruised.'

Adrian Mitchell, *Australian*

Winner 1988 National Book Council Silver Banjo Award

FOR THE BEST IN PAPERBACKS, LOOK FOR THE

PENGUIN

Shalom Compiled by Nancy Keesing

The acclaimed collection of Australian Jewish stories

Judah Waten, Alan Collins, Lilian Barnea, Serge Liberman, David Martin, Michele Nayman, Morris Lurie, Harry Marks, June Factor and many more.

Drawing on diverse backgrounds and inspirations, well-known author and critic. Nancy Keesing has selected stories showing journeys of body and spirit from Europe to Australia and back to Israel.

Some of the writers are from long-established Australian Jewish families, one dating back to the First Fleet. Others were refugees of pogroms, revolutions and wars, while some are their children, who grew up in post-war Australia.

Shalom has given telling insights into Jewish life and thought in Australia for over ten years, and become a classic. This new edition includes five more fine writers who have since emerged as major talents.

'a brilliant and moving collection . . . highly personalized vignettes which penetrate a fascinating area of life'

Australian Book Review

Lily on the Dustbin Nancy Keesing
Slang of Australian women and families

Australian families can 'talk till the cows come home'. Nancy Keesing has collected examples of hilarious and down-to-earth expressions of women and their families from all over Australia.

All the material comes from living informants, not from printed sources. Some of it is remembered from childhood—few women these days would get out the brooms and buckets for 'a good root around the house'.

Domestic slang gives a picture of Australian life which often remains private. The wit and fun of Keesing's examples are matched by the pointed, spirited drawings by Victoria Roberts.

BOOKS BY DAVID FOSTER

Dog Rock
A postal pastoral

Somewhere in the Australian countryside, not far from the city, a small and closely knit community harbours a dangerous killer. Assistant Postal Officer and Night Exchange Attendant D'Arcy D'Oliveres becomes, against his will and better judgment, inextricably tangled in the mystery. And even D'Olivres is not all he seems.

Not since *Under Milkwood* has country life been portrayed with such affection and humour. Dog Rock, not the ordinary town it appears, will haunt the memory of all who read this hilarious novel.

'a clever, zany novel whose intricate and mysterious plot . . . gives a splendid excuse for reading and savouring it again'

Nancy Keesing, *Age*

The Pale Blue Crochet Coathanger Cover
Further adventures of Dog Rock's postal detective

It's amazing what a postman has to contend with in the daily discharge of his duties. Half-deaf from the sound of his own date stamp and battling with bureaucracy (General Orders Sections 6/C/3 and 6/C/8). D'Arcy D'Oliveres is busy minding his own business, when Captain Hooch, Dog Rock's most notorious bikie, is found dead in the main display area of the Op Shop among the cushions, quilts and coathanger covers.